When Dreams Come True

St. Joseph's Lake at Notre Dame

WHEN DREAMS COME TRUE

by

Father Jan.

(Reverend Sigmund A. Jankowski C.S.C.)

NOTRE DAME, INDIANA

1970

IMPRIMATUR:
> *Most Reverend Leo A. Pursley D.D.*
> *Bishop of Fort Wayne—South Bend, Indiana.*

NIHIL OBSTAT:
> *Reverend Charles J. Corcoran C.S.C.,*
> *Censor Librorum.*

CUM PERMISSU SUPERIORUM:
> *Reverend Howard J. Kenna C.S.C.,*
> *Provincial of the Congregation of Holy Cross,*
> *Indiana Province.*

To the everlasting memory of

REVEREND STANLEY J. BIELECKI, C.S.C.
(CHEERY BILECK)

*My dear boyhood friend and companion
my fellow seminarian and my brother Priest
who died in the prime of his life
at St. Stanislaus, Bishop and Martyr, Parish
in South Bend, Indiana, on May 9th, 1930
an excellent man of God*

MAY HIS SOUL REST IN PEACE!

Chalice of Dreams

The dreams we had in childhood,
 How wonderful they were,
So full of light and laughter,
What memories they stir.

The adolescent dreaming
Was quite a different tale,
Ambitious was the vision
We found along the trail.

The dreams became more mellow
Across maturer years,
They lost a bit of laughter—
Discovering some tears.

And age will add their quota
Of dreams unto the rest;
Thruout the span of living
I wonder which were best?

Hilda Butler Farr

*When my dreams come true! When my dreams
    come true!*
*True love in all simplicity is fresh and pure as
    dew:*
*The blossom in the blackest mold is kindlier
    to the eye*
*Than any lily born of pride that looms against
    the sky;*
*And so it is I know my heart will gladly wel-
    come you,*
*When now, 'Dear Readers,' my dreams come
    true.*

James Whitcomb Riley

WORLD-FAMOUS SOUTH BEND, INDIANA, IS MY home town. It turned out to be an ideal place for a growing boy because of the presence of the University of Notre Dame. I imagine I was born with two hearts. One faded away after twenty-two years. I left it dormant like a squirrel's in wintertime, but I parted with it on a cheerful note. The other heart I took with me to Washington, D.C., to Chicago, Illinois, and back again to South Bend, Indiana, where I spent most of my years in a parish world. I have now a wealth of consoling thoughts in that I worked with souls and for souls of people of various backgrounds, most of them of Polish descent. God knows I wanted to supply them with the opportunity and the means to acquire the grace of God

1

according to my priestly vocation. May God bless them forever.

Now when I am no longer considered able to serve them, the heart I call my first one, comes freshly to life again, beating forcibly in reverse to open for me a grand panorama of my youth dreams come true. I have already made sure in my last will and testament that this original heart of mine is never to be a subject for transplanting; be it ever so humble and naive, there is no heart like my own, and it would never beat properly in somebody else's breast. I have learned from a recent newspaper column that love may flee, friendship falter and money lose its value, but memory basks best in your heart. It never lets you down. So with the deepest gratitude to Almighty God I first go to my home, and then to what in my boyhood days I loved as a Paradise on earth—Notre Dame.

When I came into this world, my home was rich in children—six girls and one boy— but rather poor otherwise. Three score and ten years ago I faced my mother for the first time. What I saw was her eyes. It was not long after that I began to love those eyes more intently. The light from them was the gleam of my mother's true and sincere faith. She was guiding my tiny arms to make the sign of the cross. To have any success with me, she had to go through many and repeated gestures, because in my awkwardness I knew nothing yet about the natural and the supernatural gifts of God, but somehow I felt that my mother, like all good mothers of her day, was planting the mustard seed of true faith in my little heart.

I saw, in turn, the jumping flame of a candlelight, the flicker of a kerosene lamp, the glow of a gas mantle and the bright flash of an electric bulb. Spaced between these at some intervals of time, I came upon the words of my first book. Father and mother taught me how to read. With their patient direction I became an avid lover of good books. My eyes were being trained also to look at nothing but what was wholesome and profitable. And here I am today still following with my eyes, though almost worn out, the beautiful things of nature outside, and besides on the inside the television with its world of wonderful pictures and sound. I see men wooing, as it were, and trying to reach the moon, after a series of rocket blasts, rides and explorations. I see an endless parade of live scenes, news, programs, all sorts of entertainments: baseball, football, basketball, golf and hockey and all other games from even as far as Hawaii, South America, Asia and Africa, to satisfy the mind and human heart. Between the original candlelight and the modern Apollos, luminous in their orbit, what miracles had man achieved with the help of Almighty God! "How manifold are your works, O Lord! In wisdom you have wrought them all." (Psalm CIII:2)

Between the log cabins and the spacecraft capsules, within less than a lifetime, one can revel in a host of dreams come true. Brilliant and hopeful fantasies, blueprints of fantastic things outlined by the genius of Leonardo da Vinci and other inventors, sprung into reality

4

to encourage in us a remarkable credence in looking forward to more and more marvelous phenomena. We welcome them, one after another, looking upon them with wonderment. "Behold the deeds of the Lord, the outstanding things He has wrought on earth" (Psalm XLV, 17–18). We lift our eyes toward heaven, and bow our heads in humble adoration and thanksgiving to the infinite goodness of the deity above.

TAKING GOOD ADVICE FROM UPRIGHT PEOPLE IS a step ahead to the upholding of religion with all your heart. Religion is not hard to grasp nor understand, if you only give it a chance. Come to think of it, it is nothing complex. In fact, it is very simple. It is something born with us, something emanating from our Creator that cannot be rubbed off completely or wiped out altogether. We have a close outright relationship to the Almighty Father in Heaven. No one can point this out to a child better than the mother. She implants the seed of faith, if she is a God-loving mother. Once there, faith must be nourished, cultivated and allowed to grow and grow to blossom some day into a tree-like myriad of branches, bearing abundant fruit of good deeds, works of charity for the bodies and the souls of our neighbors as well as of ourselves. At the bottom of it all must be solid piety, the gift of the Holy Spirit. You can admit it quite generously into your soul without fearing that someone will accuse you of displaying "pious piffle."

We sing Glory to God in the Highest to remind us of His infinite love for us in sending His only begotten Son to us through the

Virgin Mary. He revealed this truth at the beginning of the world, decorated it with the Christmas star, and later perfectly explained it for us by the hands, the eyes, and, outside of three sorrowful days, by the always and always living heart of Jesus Christ. He died for us, and on the third day of His burial he arose again from the dead. It was He who shortly after appearing before the people, did some of His friends an enormous favor at the request of His mother Mary. He blessed some drinking water, and made it blush and turn into real wine. All those who saw this miracle, the first of many He was to perform, believed that He, as Man, really came to us from heaven through the immaculate conception and the virginal birth to remain as He was from all eternity, divine. His Father confirmed this, when in the presence of Saint John, the Baptist, and throngs of people at the river Jordan, He introduced His only begotten Son by talking straight from Heaven: "This my beloved Son in whom I am well

7

pleased, hear ye him." (Matt. XVII:5). To-day this ungrateful world permeated with ideas born of the evil spirit himself, berates, insults and even ignores Christ, while His friends and disciples of this hour, who are gravely concerned about this, cry out: "Almighty Father, send us now some one like Saint John, the Baptist, to introduce the Son of God *all over again*, this time forcibly enough, to drown out the voices of unbelief, scandal and crime which are leading multitudes of men and women to the depths of hell."

You cannot ever think or say too much in favor of Christ. He is ancient and ever new. He does not age, but is ever up-to-date. He is the fashioner and the master of all the future. He is as real and as *living* as when, walking upon it, He had graced this earth. He is the alpha and omega of all time, because He is Almighty God. If you had passed Him by in your youth, and failed to recognize Him consciously or unconsciously, or, if

8

you had never read a truthful book about Him and never folded your hands to Him in prayer, *do it now*. Now is the time, now is your chance to *love* Him properly as you had never loved anybody before. He is the creator and ruler of our time, and *time* is something that runs and will run out on all of us.

In a home like mine it was the simplest thing to make Christ a daily and a living companion. It was a time-honored custom of the Polish people to praise Jesus Christ on meeting a priest or on entering their homes. "Praise be Jesus Christ!" Did you ever hear this reverential saying repeated time and again, and the answer, "Forever and ever, Amen"? If you had been a Polish boy or a Polish girl coming home, and you forgot to say this invocation, you would have to turn back on your heels, go out, close the door, come back, and say what you were supposed to say in a loud voice: "Praise be Jesus Christ!", because divine grace was at stake. There would be some one always to answer:

"Forever and ever, Amen." This together with the lovable Christmas carols and the Lenten hymns we sang, inspired a solid piety in us for the rest of our lives. Surely we meant to pass every day with at least a little show of piety, this gift of the Holy Spirit, a virtue that is slipping away from people, because they do not think supernaturally or spiritually. The love of preference for Christ, and for all that He had said must be the motivating force for activity in all homes, as it was in mine, and the commandments of God must be faithfully observed, and our neighbors never hurt deliberately.

Haley's Comet appeared in the heavens in 1910. We craned our necks to see it every evening. It was supposed to destroy the whole world. Some people got panicky as the day approached. Resigned to the will of God, we were ready to go up higher than the moon. Thinking seriously, and hoping as we were supposed to hope for a *more permanent home* after any catastrophe, we lived to see

10

the proposed "day of doom" pass by peacefully. Things went on and on as usual, and
we were on our knees saying our prayers
regularly.

OUR FAMILY WAS FURTHER BLESSED BY ONE
more girl and two brothers, who came after
me. Another youngster came upon the scene
of our home when we took in a girl who was
mercilessly driven out by her stepfather
when her mother died. She soon chose a convent, became a Sister of the Holy Cross, and
spent years in teaching children. She is now
retired and living in California.

My dear father was a man of a different calibre. He would not dream of throwing out even an adopted child like his next-door neighbor did. He had all the love and sympathy for his sons and daughters and for everybody in the neighborhood. He was a remarkably muscular man, and a jack-of-all-trades in the fullest sense of that word. I give him credit for knowing how to make almost anything. To my boyish delight, when we went out for a walk in early spring, he could with his pocket knife whittle a fine sounding whistle from a branch of a willow tree in three shakes of a sheep's tail. He was familiar with every tool known in his day, and had them all stored in our big barn. When he worked at home, we boys watched, and from him we learned the name and the use of tools, not like most of the lads of today, who do not know a chisel from a vise, because their fathers never took the trouble to show to them the proper use of tools.

My dad first applied his ingenuity to the

making of a useful and happy home. With only a minimum of book knowledge, he had the training of a German soldier which he received in Poland under the regime of Kaiser Wilhelm, and in stature and strength he looked like a first-class military man. Both he and my mother came from the part of Poland, then dominated by Germany and brought with them the treasured traditions of their own, plus whatever the Germans had to offer. Best of all they had quite a bit of formal schooling, and what was beneficial in German merged beautifully with what they learned from their Polish teachers. They were an outstanding example of this ethnic blending which they preserved intact when they came to this country.

When my dad built anything, it was here to stay. Even such an article as a good-sized sled made for us, he made so very strong, that in spite of the use and abuse it took from us, it would not break. When he fashioned an arbor for the grapes to climb on, he made it to extend from our kitchen to the barn, a good hundred feet or so, with a very tough framework to serve as a comfortable bed for the branches, and for the large leaves to shelter the luscious clusters of the berries in the fall. They were the wonder of our neighbors who were invited to share the shade on the hottest summer days, and the ripened grapes, which those on the pedlar's wagon could not match.

When Dad's hammer pounded nails into his neatly sawed boards, they were clinched so tightly and precisely that it would take nothing short of dynamite to break them up. When after a number of years expert carpenters came to wreck the annex to our kitchen which Dad had built, they were asking what mind and what hands created so simple, and yet so adroit a masterpiece. Around my home was ample room for trees, and plenty of fertile ground for a garden of no mean proportions. When I first laid my eyes upon the trees, they were pretty well grown up. The looks of them were enough to awaken in me a deep sense of admiration, but not until I read Joyce Kilmer's poem, "Trees," did they fully blossom for me, and bear an everlasting fruit of appreciation for them to be stored in my heart for all the days to come.

> *"I think that I shall never see*
> *A poem lovely as a tree.*
> *A tree whose hungry mouth is prest*
> *Against the earth's sweet flowing breast;*
> *A tree that looks at God all day,*
> *And lifts her leafy arms to pray;*
> *A tree that may in summer wear*
> *A nest of robins in her hair;*
> *Upon whose bosom snow has lain:*
> *Who intimately lives with rain.*
> *Poems are made by fools like me,*
> *But only God can make a tree.*

Trees! My Dad grew them for God and for us—all kinds, ornamental and fruit trees, pear, apple and peach trees. At least two, I remember, bore white, tasty peaches with a red tint in their meaty part, the like of which you can no longer find in this world. I have been looking for their kind for years. It is likely that they are gone forever. Oak, linden and poplar trees, sturdy all of them, stood like mighty sentinels in front of our house.

And roses: a beautiful wide fence of them, white and pink, stretched far along the lawn, separate from the rest of the garden, to make a real dream in bloom from June to November to outlast the rest of the flowers in their scattered but orderly beds.

Vegetables claimed the largest part of our garden. We had them all: onions, radishes, potatoes, carrots, turnips and parsnips; produce such as lettuce and cucumbers, tomatoes and sweet corn, popcorn and strawberries; majestic bushes loaded with raspberries, blueberries and even gooseberries. Spraying all this vegetation with chemicals was unknown to us, but we got rid of all the pests to welcome the fragrance of spring and the dew of summer into every fruit and vegetable. It was truly an adventure to pluck bugs and caterpillars off the bushes and the vines to make sure that nothing tainted the fruit to be preserved in mother's jars for fall and winter. Mother's cellar moved you to tears, when it came time to give Thanksgiving to God, and our appetites were whetted to the unfailing hope of many happy and delicious returns.

DAD RAISED EVEN TOBACCO, UNAWARE OF ITS danger. I saw him gather its extra large leaves to be dried in the attic, and then pulverized in his improvised iron crock and masher. He knew how to make fragrant tobacco for his pipe and snuff for his sneezing.

17

Sometimes he raised himself on his toes to a disproportionate sneeze so as to scare us with a bang. It sounded almost like a volcanic eruption. When autumn came around, and the corn was shucked, he made pipes out of corn cobs and fancy snuff boxes from the horns of a bull, not forgetting to engrave neatly the proper name of his friend for whom this sniffy receptacle was meant.

While I am on the subject of tobacco, smoking comes to my mind. Why do so many people dim their faces, and sniff tobacco under their noses? They fall for what may prove a decided drawback to their physical welfare. They think nothing of it, and yet to smoke, to breathe God's pure air through a cigar, pipe or a cigarette; to pollute the atmosphere, as it were, smacks of something unfair to the human make-up. I was foolish enough to try it for a very short time. I smoked, and once or twice I chewed tobacco. I shook off, however, any semblance of a habit, and forestalled an obnoxious progress in life.

Nicotine has been the tempting and insistent culprit in the world. It is one of the worst poisons in existence. By inhaling it through smoking, fair maidens of our time, beautiful girls, ruin and lose their natural beauty. Young men invite to themselves scrubby wrinkles and haggard looks way ahead of their age by smoking and chewing tobacco. "Do you want to live longer?" Let an esteemed professor of physiology and biology at Notre Dame of long ago answer this question. Only two words of his will cover it. *"DON'T SMOKE!"* Go along with the professor. He is still living, and pushing almost a hundred years. "Don't smoke." It would take pages to explain this prohibition. It can be very brief, however. It is intimately linked with the Fifth Commandment, "Thou shalt not kill." Do not jeopardize your God-given health. No matter how you look at it, if you use tobacco, the evidence is against you. Many people have injured their physical well being, and some fatally, by smoking and chewing.

I remember how this professor at Notre

Dame laid down the truth and the law before us. The structure of our bodies is composed of tiny cells, each and every one all important, kept alive and healthy through the initial blood given us by our good fathers and mothers from the moment of our conception to our birth. Our cells were then becoming sound, nurtured by our own blood, which was being distilled from proper and wholesome food by our wonderful digestive process. The perfect order and the union in their growth and multiplication was never meant by God to be disturbed by any poison whatsoever. Allow nicotine to ooze out of smoking by inhaling or swallowing it with the saliva contaminated by the chewed tobacco, and you cause a toxic reaction. A cell may be sickened by the one next to it, and so on and on, and in time an ulcer is formed. The ulcer, whose growth is imminent, most difficult to check, may slowly become malignant, and ultimately becomes the killer, cancer.

It took our government almost one hundred and eighty-five years to put its finger on this unfortunate menace plaguing our population. When the blessed news of staving off tobacco smoking and chewing came, it flashed upon me a timely coincidence. The headlines proclaiming the discovery of the harm caused by tobacco rang true to my old professor's words: "Do you want to live long? Don't smoke. Don't chew tobacco." That was right out of the venerable gentleman's mouth, except that the government now adds this caution: "If you don't smoke or chew, don't start. If you do, quit. Don't be a loser." Of all the sad things that can be said about a man or a woman, the saddest is "they smoked like chimneys, and coughed like bears."

Because smoking and chewing are closely allied to the habit of excessive drinking of alcoholic beverages, my blessed home supplied us with a useful counter remedy. Beer, whiskey, wine and the like were there in the house for the older folks, but always with the label of moderate dosage from dad and mom; so much and no more. But even we growing children got a little swig of beer, a tiny jigger of wine and a wee bit of whiskey or brandy as a medicine; sometimes a more generous dash or two for the holding of it on a toothache with the prescription and the strict orders not to swallow it, but to spit it out as soon as the tooth got numb or stopped aching. At any rate the quality of the whiskey was so good that it would not burn your mouth inside out, bend your ears or smart your eyes. We learned very early in life that a little, and not too much alcohol was excellent for the human system. It was perfectly excusable for us, if on the occasion of a toothache, we swallowed the forbidden juice against all rules. The apathy towards hard drinks remains forever in our minds, while dad's and mom's dosage stands also pat for the rest of our lives: "A little bit at a time will do no harm, and will drag you away farther and farther from the devil's drunken charm."

The following news report will illustrate what a height of stupidity a drunkard can attain. In a very old village in this country a man died. It was December and extremely cold. Someone had to dig the grave. A rugged fellow volunteered to do the job. For his tools he took a pick and two shovels. He set out to work, and soon broke through the thick crust of the frozen earth. He kept on digging, digging and digging. Whistling a tune, he kept quite warm, and forgot what he was doing, until he woke up to the fact that, digging, he found himself in the ground far below the required depth of the grave. There was no way of climbing out. The extra shovel lay idle on top. Perplexed, he slowly began to freeze and freeze hard. All he could do was to shout to high heaven for help. Raising his voice, he called: "Help, Help! Help! I am freezing to death. I can't get out. Help! Help!" Echoes only bounced from the adjoining hills, and rolled among the tombstones. The rustle of the trees and dead silence contributed to the freezing man's anguish. Suddenly, as if out of nowhere appeared a figure of what, we would say, was a promise of rescue. It was not a ghost, but a confirmed drunkard who happened to be passing by the cemetery. He had heard the frantic cries: "Help! Help!!" Who could be shouting here? "They are all supposed to be dead." He cocked his ear, and with his halting footsteps struck the right direction. His bleary eyes doubled their size, and just about popped out, when he came upon the open grave with a man in it alive. It was too much for the toper to solve this drastic situation, so his wits went altogether awry. Paying no attention to the desperate cries, he mumbled: "No wonder you are cold and freezing. You aren't covered, and everybody in this cemetery ought to be covered." Thereupon he seized the extra shovel, and began piling the earth right on top of the hapless and praying victim way below. Despite his frantic begging to stop, that son of Bacchus kept shoveling and shoveling on, until he buried the grave-digger alive. All finished, he threw the shovel aside, wiped the perspiration from his brow with a huge red handkerchief, and with a sigh of relief, doffed his hat, and proceeded to stagger his way home, whispering: "May he rest in peace!", perfectly satisfied that he had done a "noble work of mercy." What happened after this, your guess is as good as mine. In very, very ancient times Seneca had already said: "Drunkenness is nothing else but a voluntary madness."

BEYOND HIS KINDLY SUPERVISION OVER HIS household, my Dad worked ten hours a day at the old Oliver Factory, where horse-driven plows were made. Mother and we kids kept his garden in trim during the bright summer days. You could see us armed with pinchers and tin cans, usually salmon cans, the only ones we had, to go after the bugs on the potato, tomato and cabbage plants as well as the caterpillars on the wide leaves of the grape producing vines. We left our vegetables and fruit to be dressed not by pests and parasites but by the rain and sunshine in splendor without a flaw, and in fragrance sweet enough to tempt any king's or a queen's taste without measure. In this particular location we happened to be the royalty, very much blessed by the King of Kings.

"Man goes to his work and to his tillage till the evening." (Psalm CIII:2). If there were anyone who fulfilled this scriptural passage right on the button, it was my father. Every morning, Monday through Saturday, you could see him walking regularly to the factory at least a good mile away. Once at his post, he would pick up a pair of lengthy tongs with his hardened hand to grip a piece of raw iron which he would place into a flaming furnace. He would pull out this plate now red hot to set it on a form below. In a jiffy he tripped a huge hammer from above, and struck a plowshare from the mold. Amid sparks, flames and steam, the red-hot blades were cooled off one by one in a water keg. Conveyers moved them on to the emery wheels to make them sharp and shiny. The silvery plow shares were then attached to their wooden skeletons to make these famous implements, the pride of many a farmer.

They were sturdy and cheerful pioneers of all nationalities, perspiring and even a little scorched, inured to hardship and heat by hard labor without a complaint. Incessant bearing up and spirit like this helped to build our beautiful United States of America. Between the sounds of a sonorous factory whistle, no man yielded a minute, even at the point of near exhaustion, as the new plows were rolling out to be guided back of the horses by the hands of our farmers. The factory workers were paid, yes, they were paid to the amount of about sixteen dollars and a few cents a week. Money was worth a great deal more then, and with honest frugality and sacrifice most men made ends meet. My Dad usually had surplus of a few shiny pennies jingling in his pay envelope. These were always in reserve for us in exchange for a great big hug.

Without the least pouting ever we were doing our Dad a daily favor. We fetched his lunch basket every noon. As soon as one attained the age of nine, he took his turn. I followed my sisters and brother, hurrying to the factory shortly before the lunch hour. Sometimes I was a little ahead of time to catch the men still working. The deafening noise of the dropping hammers was not exactly music, but it was fascinating to my ears. The sparks flying all around from the spinning emery wheels flashed before me like a giant display of sparklers on the Fourth of July. I liked that too.

When the whistle blew, my Dad dropped the tongs, washed his hands and waved to me standing with googly eyes a few yards away. He came quickly to claim his lunch. I remember how he put his strong right arm around my shoulder, and said lovingly: "See, my son, I work so hard that you and all my boys will not have to, when you grow up." It was then that my Dad looked to me like a giant of good, a hero, truly like the right hand of Almighty God Himself. His dream came true, but he did not see it all the way. He died when I was fifteen. My older brother became a successful architect, my other two brothers printers, and I was ordained a priest of the Congregation of Holy Cross. He intended to instil into the veins of his sons with discipline and sacrifice at any cost, the punctuality, the will to be exact, always to do the right thing, his patience and courage that were his fine traits.

After coming home from the factory in the evening, he had enough strength left to continue his labor of love for us. He went forth to his tillage. He kept working in the garden until the last vestige of daylight faded away. Satisfied that all was in tip-top shape around our little municipal farm and barn, he saw to it that the chickens, ducks and geese were fed, and gone to roost. He returned to his room for a few hours of a well earned rest, but not before he would kneel at his bedside to say his prayers. Just at this moment I dared to peek in his room. I saw him in that pious position, and I heard the whispers of his talk to God. I felt as if he were carving a statue of Saint Joseph in my heart. On restful days like Sundays, dressed like Beau Brummel he went off to church to Mass and to Holy Communion. On Election Day he looked like a senator in his dark suit and his broad-brimmed hat, as he went to cast his vote for his political favorite, Colonel Teddy Roosevelt, whom he held in great esteem.

AND NOW MY MOTHER! HER FACE ALWAYS WORE a determined, but pleasant and close to a very cheerful expression. Her almost jet-black hair fell over her shoulders in long tresses. I, as a tot standing behind her rocker, whenever her locks were loose, loved to stroke and comb them up and down. She was bright, bonnie-eyed and cherry-lipped to me, a woman full of common sense, and after a fashion, in my judgement, an image of the prayerful Handmaid of the Lord. She made a grand and excellent housekeeper. From first to last our home was scrupulously clean. Helter-skelterness was always taboo. When flies were prolific in summertime, Mom would chase the very last of them to catch it dead or alive. We played outside of the house within earshot for her melodious call. But, if you were a boy of ten, and made yourself a neat and good-sized kite and had it flying high up in the heavens, letting out all the possible string you had, till only a speck of that kite was showing to your proud and happy eyes, boasting, of course, that no one ever had a kite up that high, while all the kids in the neighborhood stood around you in admiration and congratulation; you stood your ground as the sole possessor and pilot of this masterpiece, as long as you hung on to the end of the string. And then you heard your mother calling you home to do a chore. Call after call would come my way louder and clearer. I shut off my ears. I would not think of entrusting my hold of that kite to any one in this world. But I was disobeying mother, when all at once, as if out of nowhere, came one of my darling sisters with a pair of scissors and cut the string in my hands. The life-line was gone. My kite went somewhere into utter oblivion. My champion ended its flight right there, and forever. I burst into tears, but they did no good except eased my panic. They could not bring back my kite. They just planted in my head a strong spiritual lesson against pride and disobedience.

It is no use trying to get ahead of God-loving mothers. They seldom sleep, when you do. After working a little, playing much base-ball, cavorting and romping about till it got dark, I came home one summer night not too late, but very, very tired. Thoughtlessly I threw myself on my bed, and fell hard asleep without kneeling down and saying my prayers. I thought I was dreaming when someone pulled my leg to tumble me out of bed. My mother was standing beside at attention like Saint Joan of Arc. For what purpose? It soon dawned on me: "No one is to go to bed in this house without saying his prayers." A bit groggy still, I steadied myself on my knees, and began mumbling something to Our Father in Heaven. For mother this would not do, so a cuff on my ear taught me forever that one has to be in good shape and proper mood to talk to one's God and Saviour.

My mother specialized in common sense. Beyond all poetry, music and art and everything you can imagine, the greatest thing in life for her was the grace of God. In it she passed her days with a peaceful conscience. She loved people more than books. In fact, she never read a cook book, but how she could manage, operate and replenish the kitchen, and prepare such gorgeous meals! The art of cooking came to her naturally. She brought it with her as a young and beautiful girl from across the ocean. With unmatched skill she prepared and spread the variegated and wonderful Polish cuisine. Besides the daily menu of fresh and substantial food, she baked cakes, pies, bread and doughnuts especially for Sunday and the holidays. Those doughnuts looked like good-sized snowballs with their powdered sugar coats. With the dough, and a secret process of raising the dough, she mixed the greatest ingredient of them all, her mother love, which never could escape, because these doughnuts had no holes. Round and puff-like they were, and she would make so many that our stomachs were too small to dispose of them all. We shared them with our grateful friends and neighbors. My sisters under her mild tutelage all lived to become excellent housekeepers and magnificent cooks themselves.

My mother, an untiring worker, took time out to visit the sick and do acts of charity. You could see her walking, calm and always even-tempered, well dressed in neatly ironed clothes, often stopping to give attention to children, while she made her way to the homes of relatives and friends. At no time did I see her ruffled, angry or engaged in idle gossip. When she died, she was painfully missed. She lived nine years after my father died. Neither of my parents saw me a priest. The joy that comes to a father and a mother on their son's ordination day was shared by my brothers and sisters, but to my parents it was, and I hope it remains, a jewel in their crown in heaven.

When as a theologian I came from Washington, D.C. for my mother's funeral, and stood at her coffin at home, a middle-aged man, unknown to me, walked in to pay his respects for the last time, and made this remark without any hint or provocation from anyone. "This," he said with what seemed all the love and appreciation of our neighborhood, "is a lady who never hurt anybody." This short and perfect eulogy from my new friend settled upon my heart like a lot of cream of the human kindness coming to us by way of sympathy from all the good people around us. At one time I ran across a similar expression in the famous Cardinal John Henry Newman's, "Idea of a University," where he wrote that it is almost a definition of a gentleman that he is one who never inflicts pain. I was glad to apply this passage to my mother who was a gentlewoman, and I blessed the gentleman who voiced this epitaph for my dearest mother: "She was one who never inflicted pain."

In heaven what must mother be,
On earth my shining prize held she
On the rainbow's end of childhood;
And oh, how she there stood
An angel of good!
No farther than her heart for me
Was the lure of my dreams' reality.
From her firmest guardian hold
God's truth, the living Faith, she passed on
  to me.

*

True motherhood, how brightly it ends,
And higher than the rainbow bends
Her prayer and bliss remain above

With God, her eternal gain.
Fancy you the worth of a mother's crown,
Think how Lucifer, once threatening, fallen
  down
With pride, twisted his archangelic face to a
  fearful frown,
And was crushed beneath Her, the one and only
  Virgin Love.

✳

Before I leave my mother, this memento
concerning her is not the least to bear re-
counting. From time to time in my childhood
she would point out to me a picture hanging
in my bedroom. It was "The Apparition of
Our Lady at Lourdes." This occasioned another blessed dream for me, rising to be true
somewhere in far-off reality. It cleared for
me the way to Notre Dame, for on my first
visit there, I screwed my heart to the Grotto
of Lourdes. Years later, when I had already
seen the original Shrine at Lourdes itself, I
hit upon the idea of building a Grotto for the
people in my pastoral days at the Church of

St. Stanislaus, Bishop and Martyr, in South Bend. Discovering heaps of stone out in the country, and depending much on the good will of a generous old farmer, I gathered the precious materials with the kind help of others. I was fortunate to find an expert stone mason who, himself a protestant, cheerfully accepted the job, and showed a remarkable interest in the project. He laid rock upon rock so meticulously and faithfully that in a short time a replica of the Grottos at Lourdes and at Notre Dame became a reality before the eyes of those who truly love the Blessed Mother of God. This too was my labor of love for the Virgin Lady, the fulfillment of my long cherished dream. When I reached my sixty-seventh year less three months, I lay in St. Joseph Hospital in South Bend, stricken with some kind of a malady. Fallen out of bed, and unconscious I was ignored as a hopeless case by an unscrupulous and careless nurse on duty who told her co-worker that I had only a few minutes to live. This other more conscientious nurse, who told me this story, thought otherwise. If she had not hurried to help me, I would have turned my toes up to the daisies right there and then, and nobody in the world would ever know why I passed away. As it happened, the Immaculate Heart of Mary, Our Lady of Lourdes intervened. The beautiful soul of that nurse, who learned of my miserable plight from the one who mercilessly and uncharitably passed me by, took the tip from the Mother of God to her blessed heart, and found me just in time. She secured help to lift me off the floor, summoned two doctors who immediately took me to the operating room to open my head. Besides correcting the mal-function, they with supernatural help, as one of them told me some days after, declared the gray matter to be sound in that cranium of mine, and guaranteed it to be intact.

How very wonderful it is to be a priest. In my illness, even in the beginning my fel-

Grotto at St. Stanislaus Parish, South Bend

41

low priests, brothers and sisters, my relatives and friends, children and all my parishioners stormed heaven for me. Our Blessed Mother, mindful of their prayers plus the excellent quality of my blood inherited from my parents, supplied the remedy and helped the miracle. A priest was allowed to go on living. I forgive the questionable nurse, who in my case failed to imitate the Good Samaritan. As to the Queen of Heaven, never anyone pass her by. Get all enthused about her and be always proud of her. *Cling to your holy beads!*

CONSTANT AND SPIRITED CONVERSATION OF THE boys about daily round-the-world sports often irked our older sisters at home, but we explained sometimes kindly and sometimes roguishly that girls were meant for the kitchen and housework and we huskies for athletics. We loved all the winners in sports. We were hero worshippers long before we knew the meaning of the term. Baseball and football stars, champion automobile racers, hockey players and prize-fighters were the idols of our day. Pictures cut out of newspapers and magazines and from anywhere we could find them decked the walls of our barn. This was our continuous sports parade. We played a lot of baseball, not achieving any remarkable prowess in the game, but we held our own with the kids. We could tell the standings, the scores and the averages of most of the players right off the bat in the big leagues as well as in the Central, a minor league, in which South Bend was a member team. My mother often quipped that we knew sports better than our prayers. I walked to Springbrook Park near Mishawaka, Indiana, nearly five miles away from my home to see South

Bend play, even if I had to look through a knot hole in the big wooden fence till the seventh inning. We were then allowed to walk into the park minus a ticket. Once at the very start of the game, I got a boost from a tall chum of mine, and jumped over the fence, but lo and behold, to my great surprise, I landed straight into the arms of a policeman. I was more fortunate later, when as a young man I walked into the ball park in Washington, D.C. an extremely proud fan to see Walter Johnson pitch one of his last games. As the years went by, in Chicago, where I was stationed for eight years, I witnessed Babe Ruth, Lou Gehrig and Hank Wilson hit some of their prodigious home runs, and Jack Johnson and Jess Willard flatten the noses of their opponents.

But my outstanding interest in early boyhood days really blossomed into a passion for circuses. Winter months seemed to pass by quickly in anticipation of Ringling Brothers, Barnum and Bailey, Hagenbeck and Wal-

The Circus is coming!
Photos—Courtesy of the South Bend Tribune and Mr. Bruce
Harlan, Photographer, University of Notre Dame

lace, Sells Floto, Robinson, Buffalo Bill and 101 Ranch Circuses and Wild West Shows. They visited South Bend in periodical rotation. I got to know them all. Nothing could make the sun shine brighter for me than these living exhibitions of railroad and tent extravaganzas, spreading on the grounds of Oliver Field and Prairie Avenue. I prayed so that the circus would not strike a school day, and it seemed that heaven favored it to come most of the time during our vacation. I set out early on the appointed date to see swarthy men unload all the grand paraphernalia from gaudily painted railroad cars—horses, elephants, camels, zebras, tents and poles and canvasses, systematically piled and bundled to be set in place. Fine looking and strong horses and elephants pulled the picturesque parade and other wagons. Most amusing were the burly negroes grouped around the tent stakes, who rhythmically pounded them into ground with large sledge hammers. Different crews of workers fastened the ropes, while the tents went up, and the negroes, swinging their hammers, went from one tent to another amid a volley of their own songs: "Ole Black Joe," "Swanee River," "Dixie" and the like. Those mirthful blackmen were a performance in themselves.

Outdoor circuses demanded very many chores and there was at once a call for boy volunteers. I was on the spot more quickly and eagerly than I ever was at home. The reward was an admission ticket, and it looked like the Big Top itself with all the show. My assignment was to water the elephants, and I wasted no time. Two buckets filled with water dangled heavily from my arms as I trudged my elephant-way to and from the hydrant. How many elephants were there? Too many. They drank not like fish, but like whales, as I fetched the water almost to a point of exhaustion. I figured that elephants must have humps like camels, only they are like huge elastic drums hidden by a thick layer of black skin. I never saw a white elephant or a pink one. If there be creatures of this kind, trainers must paint them white or pink.

My dull and heavy parade seemed miles long. I thought it would never end. But with the ticket to the Big Top almost in my pocket, and the bands striking up high, my elephant parade ended on a delightful note. The big circus parade was forming. This was something "right up my alley," and I ran to get a good place at the street curb to see the grandest of grand marches in the world, The Circus Parade, as James Whitcomb Riley, the Poet, saw it:

"Oh! the Circus Day Parade!
How the bugles played and played!
And how the glossy horses tossed their flossy
manes and neighed,
As the rattle and the rhyme of the tenor-
drummer's time
Felled all the hungry hearts of us with mel-
ody sublime!

How the graceless—graceful stride of the elephants was eyed,

And the capers of the little horse that can-
tered at their side!
How the shambling camels, tame to the plaudits of their fame,
With listless eyes came silent, masticating as
they came.

How the cages jolted past, with each wagon
battened fast,
And the mystery within it only hinted of at
last
From the little grated square in the rear, and
nosing there
The snout of some strange animal that sniffed
the outer air!

And, last of all, THE CLOWN, making mirth
for all the town,
With his lip curved ever upward and his eye-
brows ever down,
And his chief attention paid to the little mule
that played
A tatoo on the dashboard with his heels, in
the Parade."

Ringling Brothers boasted of a famous
clown who rode his dilapidated velocipede
up and down the avenue as the parade kept

49

marching on. He barely skipped our toes as we tempted him to run them down. I envied Happy Hooligan. Why could not I be a clown? I was mischievous enough. I would have been, if it were not for the grace of God. I would not have been the Ringmaster, but just a clown. When I was leaving for the priesthood, all my dear ones concerned were laughing. They would not believe it. I was the only one who was crying.

Going back to the circus, I have always retained my love for the clowns. They are the easiest people to get along with. To put my hand into a Clown's hand always tickled me. I wondered if clowns ever suffer, or have any troubles at all with all the fun they make for the rest of us. Let me tell you something. A man, a perfect stranger in town, walked into a doctor's office late in the evening on a circus day. He was nervous, fidgety and headachy and for all that, very, very melancholy. The doctor who had been at the circus that afternoon, faced his patient with the broadest smile that had ever widened his face. He was still gloating over what he happily saw under the Big Top. "What a performance! What clowns! What antics!" His caller kept silent, sad, gloomy, dejected like one ready to commit suicide. The doctor went on: "What man? Nonsense! Circus is in town! Go to the grounds! Go to Coco, the Clown. He's an antidote for whatever ails you. Cheer up!" The rampaging enthusiasm of the doctor for Coco stifled in him any chance to make proper diagnosis for his gloomy patient. "I will take you to Coco, the Clown, tonight, all right?" At that came the quiet answer: *"I am Coco, The Clown."* The doctor lost his balance, fell out of his chair, and fainted away. Who said clowns have no troubles? Go ahead, Coco, take care of the doctor, for according to him you can be both a physician and a clown.

8

MY GRADE SCHOOL YEARS WERE THOSE OF AN average American boy, walking every day back and forth. Cars were scarce in those days. The distance between home and school was over a mile, but even the deepest snow would not keep boys and girls from going. A school day was a thorough school day, very important, and we hardly ever lost one. We were well instructed as to how to behave in the classroom. Sister teacher stood there in place of Dad and Mom under whose remote supervision I was there to learn all there was to retain in my head, and bring to my ever strictly school-upholding and seconding home. The springtime of my life was unfolding itself in prayer, reading, serving Holy Mass and singing, running errands for mother, flying kites and playing ball in summer, skating and hopping bobsleds in winter, not worrying whether or how soon my parents would buy me an automobile; but worrying about my studies and grades, delivering newspapers; proud to give Mom my little pay, sporting a black eye now and then, because of a little impromptu boxing minus gloves, when tempers flaired; and sometimes just doing nothing, but dreaming and wasting time.

One thing I did with real gusto was to read the History of the United States. I loved all the books I could find about our explorers, settlers, colonists and pioneers. And what a privilege it was to rent books from the public library without any charge! To me it was almost unbelieveable, as I became a glutton for books. I perused the pages of events and stories leading up to the wonderful make-up of this country from the Star Spangled Banner of Francis Scott Key to the Rough Riders of Teddy Roosevelt and thereafter. What a wealth of inspiration and splendid examples of nobility proceed from the flag of the United States, the array of historical characters and events which are enough for any serious-minded lad or lassie to stir in them the ambition to make true Americans of themselves!

Too many of our boys and girls frown on American History. They pass it off with little interest and love for it. Any amount of books covering the periods from the Valley Forge of Washington to the Log Cabin of Lincoln, and from there on up to date, show the intrepid spirit and the indomitable courage of our leaders of the past. Pages upon pages tell of the arduous struggle of our settlers, the trail-blazing covered wagons of the pioneers, and of all heroic men and women who came after them, fighting for the right with tears and blood. With unselfish labor they applied their genius to building and invention of many things which brought prosperity, beauty and peace to all present and future citizens. Just look around, observe and reflect upon the handy and useful things in this country—the one and indivisible nation, under God, with liberty and justice for all. The Flag of the United States does honor to it, as it stands beautifully, and waves proudly in the breeze with its silent eloquence to urge every boy and girl to take ample stock in the history of their prodigious homeland. Go forward then. Go on a path strewn with roses for you, and do not mind the thorns—they must be there. But go not in age only, not in any shallow or questionable knowledge, but in the far-seeing wisdom of our forefathers. You will find it, as they did, proceeding first and foremost from a living faith in the existence of a personal God and His providence.

"Ask not what your country can do for you, —ask what you can do for your country."— Take this guiding and blessed advice from a man who had been a courageous, intensely American President. Honor him daily and pray for his soul. He was a veteran of the

Armed Forces, who, while in office as president, the 35th in line for the United States, *gave his life for his country in 1963,—John Fitzgerald Kennedy of happy memory for all time.*

From a palace of dreams or from an air castle, not through any choice of my own, came into my boyhood life a typical American. She was one of the many hidden and unknown. She was a lady educated in the quiet and obscure confines of a convent. Distinguished already in her name, as Sister Mary Christella of the Congregation of Holy Cross, she was forever in my life a Christella. This means the Star of Christ. She was a teacher in my elementary school—a gentle ruler of the seventh grade. She honored her classroom with a title no less than her Little Kingdom of God in partnership with Uncle Sam. John Milton, the poet, would describe her best: "Grace was in her steps, and heaven in her eyes; in every gesture of hers, there was dignity and love for all." Faith, hope and charity emanated from her mind and heart to brighten and confirm every truth she was revealing to us. She had led us into a land of dreams with a promise of reality ahead. She may have had Christ himself hidden as a boy in her classroom, for her presentations of the mysteries of our faith darted like arrows into our heads and hearts and fixed them there clear and strong for good.

I found Sister Christella once holding a picture of a Christian martyr kneeling beside what looked like a ferocious leopard in the Coliseum in Rome. She unfolded for me the story of a life dedicated to the truth of Christ, in defense of which this young man was about to be torn to pieces by the wild animal in the pagan persecutions centuries ago in Rome. But as it came to pass the beast suddenly and miraculously became as gentle as a lamb and did the saintly captive no harm. The picture with its holy theme drilled itself beautifully and hopefully into my series of dreams, and I imagined it possible for me to be some day in the Coliseum in Rome. Forty years later, I found myself there not in any heroic role nor with a big live leopard at my side, but kneeling alone perhaps on the same spot as the martyr-to-be of long, long ago.

Opening a book on the history of the United States, Sister Christella turned to an attractive print of the Capitol Building in Washingon, D.C. "How would you like to be standing way high on these steps, looking up clear to the flag waving from that large and precious dome?" I stretched my eyes far into my dream world again, and as time marched on, the Capitol in Washington blazed in all its patriotic glory right before me, standing on its time-honored and time-trodden steps. At this sweet and happy moment of my life I thanked God for my dream come true, and for Sister Christella. Truly she had been training young minds for the greater things of life. Sisters like her must come from the rank and file of honest-thinking and self-sacrificing girlhood brought up in pious homes where the religious vocations are certainly and almost exclusively born. Otherwise we will not even budge and dispel the now crying need of God's devoted Sisters to fill the wide and dreadful gap in our schools. "They that instruct many to justice, shall shine as stars for all eternity." (Daniel XII:31). Shine on, Christ's Star—Sister M. Christella!

9

MY OVER-ALL LOOK OF NOTRE DAME DATES TO the age of seven. It was then that I tagged along with my sisters, two other girls and a gentleman, our relatives from Grand Rapids,

Michigan. Brother Victor, a religious of Holy Cross, served as our guide. Humble, genial and generous he was quick to endear himself to a boy like me. Holding on to his profession cord, I kept close to him to catch every word he was saying. We went to Sacred Heart Church. In its precious and colorful interior my eyes were attracted most to the Stations of the Cross, especially to the fourth. Now after many years, I notice that this station which had given so much solace and love to those facing it with devotion and prayer, and all the other stations, followed one by one for the accumulation of God's wonderful grace in the making of the Way of the Cross, have been unceremoniously removed. One wonders why. How anyone could get rid of these precious works of art from their proper places is beyond humble yet curious comprehension. They can not be seen any more. If they be not restored, but surrendered to oblivion, it will be an insult to Our Lord himself and a blotch upon the memory of Dom Gregori, the painter and artist who left the fulness of his genius to God and to all the sons of Notre Dame forevermore.

In one of the side chapels the relics of Saint Severa, prettily dressed from her veil to her sandals, greatly stirred my soul-leaping emotions. She was the Virgin who was murdered by her pagan father way back in the Christian persecutions of ancient Rome for receiving her First Holy Communion. Just now the replica of her spotless body, showing the fatal wound, became an unusual and sweet memorandum to hold on to for a boy who was being prepared for his own First Communion Day. I was feeling sorry that little Severa did not have a father like my own.

The good Brother then took us to the big Gymnasium. There for the first time I saw an aeroplane in the making. I was not much impressed. To me it looked like something clumsy and cumbersome that even the Angels could not lift up to the sky. But somebody thought otherwise. The genius of Dr.

Aerial View, University of Notre Dame

62

Albert Zahm was behind this new project. This original plane, after the pattern set by the Wright Brothers in Dayton, Ohio, after many preparations and trials, took off successfully from the ground, and it was not long after that planes began flying everywhere, and even over Notre Dame. There was peace, however, on land and sea, and in the air. But the war came, as wars must come. The Wright Brothers and Dr. Zahm expressed their regrets that what they invented was put to drastic use of hurtling deadly bombs on human beings. Bombers began to multiply, spreading fire, destruction and havoc among military installations and innocent folk with a terrific loss of life and homes in cities, and random chosen targets. A sad and bloody pall dropped over the wonderfully developed and otherwise very productive science of aeronautics.

The subject of aeroplanes recalls for me this rather pleasant incident. A two-seater flying machine landed at Notre Dame one

Friday afternoon. The pilot was an alumnus, and offered us a ride. Nobody in a curious crowd that had gathered could summon up enough courage to go flying except Brother Gilbert among us, who weighed every bit of four hundred pounds. For Brothers it was a religious rule not to leave the premises without the knowledge of the proper authority, but this Brother, being air-minded and daring, jumped at the idea of an altogether new ride, and filled to the fullest extent the narrow seat in the plane. We got apprehensive of his health and safety as the plane took off. The flight over Notre Dame was clocked to last about fifteen minutes, and Brother Gilbert, the heaviest of our heavyweights, waving to us triumphantly, came down safely and slowly loosed himself out of the plane, happy and as sound as a whistle. But he resorted to defy us all. To justify his ride, and to clear his conscience, he pronounced himself guilty. That evening very penitentially at a religious exercise before the rest of the

Brothers, he accused himself of *Leaving The Ground Without Permission.*

With Brother Victor's hand clasped in mine, I walked with the other visitors toward the Main Building, curious as to what was there under the big dome. We entered below the front stairs, and the large double doors opened into spacious dining rooms for the students. It was vacation and no meal time, so hardly any soul was there. We then trudged laboriously up the stairs to the last floor under the dome and found ourselves in the Art Rooms with their sculptures and paintings and student workshops. We viewed the adjoining large University Library, which was called the Lemmonier Library after a distinguished father of the Congregation of Holy Cross, the first Librarian. We came down to a number of classrooms on the first and the second floor, and in one of them Brother Victor lifted me up into a row of students' desks, and planted me in a seat, saying: "Some day, Boy, you will be sitting

65

right here before a Professor with big eyes and big glasses." His prophecy came true. In that very place which I proudly occupied for a moment, seven years later I faced with some intelligence old Professor James Hines of happy memory, trying to absorb some facts in Ancient History expounded by this lovable man who was stern, but truly sympathetic to all his students.

Walking out of the main entrance of the domed building, we faced the beautiful array of trees, the magnificent flower beds and the variety of shrubs glorious in their verdure and bloom of summertime at Notre Dame. This was also a fine sanctuary for the birds. You could see practically every bird known in the United States, romping around, nesting and singing beautifully to your heart's content. To the right of us paralleled the ivy-covered church, hiding the Presbytery, and a little ways around it the Grotto of Lourdes as it is now. In the silent meditation with my dear ones at my side I felt one more dream,

Administration Building, University of Notre Dame

a rosy invitation to come some day and stay at Notre Dame. The thoughts of youth, said the poet Longfellow, are long, long thoughts, and mine were reaching all the way across six years to set my anchor at Our Lady's place.

I was twelve, when I appeared around these now familiar and cherished scenes, but not officially yet, for I had a year to wait. I came just to see a baseball game between Notre Dame and Michigan. I hopped off my bicycle at the gate of Cartier Field. I had no admission money. I was hanging around, hoping. The gate tender was a student who caught my beggarly eye. When everybody had gone in, just the two of us were left at the gate, looking at each other, the fellow with the big Monogram N.D., and I with my Huckleberry Finn pants. He motioned me in. His name was Paul "Curly" Nowers, and from this moment on, my friend and my hero. Leaving my bike at the gate, I was escorted to the grandstand, and thanks to Mr. Nowers, feeling all the way like a Little Notre Dame Man. I enjoyed many sport events' meetings since that first baseball game with Curly Nowers, but unfortunately World War I broke out, and he had to leave Notre Dame to join the armed forces. I parted with him, promising him to put a red star out in the window of my home to honor his volunteer service. I told him I would have liked to pluck a real star out of the sky for him, but he had a better idea by saying to me just to leave that extra star shining for him up there from Heaven, next to Our Lord's Christmas Service Star. He, like an extra Wise Man would try to find Him there. It was not long that Curly actually did so. He was killed in action on the European battlefront in World War I. I changed his red star to a gold star to match his own shining in the heavens above. The name of Paul Nowers appears on the Memorial Tablet at the east entrance of Sacred Heart Church among those who have made the supreme sacrifice for God, country and Notre Dame. May he and his fellow-heroes through the mercy of God, rest in peace, for they were all good Notre Dame Men.

With a grade-school diploma tucked under my arm, and a bouquet of roses from my folks, I was graduated from St. Hedwige School in June, 1913. Three months later, like an eager eaglet, I swooped down on Notre Dame for good with the nest of my collection of dreams. Entering Notre Dame was like facing a bright morning summer sunshine with all roads open to make all my blessed dreams real. Father Thomas Irving officially enrolled me. I felt now that I owned at least half of the world. I walked out, and looked high up to the steeple of Sacred Heart Church pointing straight to God. It was for me the image of religion in all its totality. Next to it, majestically rising, was the Golden Dome which for me outlined the knowledge and the science I came here to learn. Not the least in prominence a little farther away loomed a tall active chimney, curling its heavy smoke into the clean air to remind me that no one ever got to heaven without working hard. Last of all I saluted the greatest symbol of all, our Blessed Lady on the dome. This is the golden image which identifies Notre Dame in full, and has inspired meditation such as this from the heart and pen of our Charles L. O'Donnell, C.S.C.

A PRAYER

The August moonlight silvers all the dome!
How many summers thus? what lifted eyes—
That since have known beginning of their peace
In gazing on one Face—have gleaned this sight?
How many shall, when mine perchance have met
The fadeless Vision?

Pray God, until the moon
Is made the fixèd footstool of her feet,
And all the stars, compact in golden twelve,
Shall glimmer deathless round her perfect brow,
May Mary stand 'twixt heaven and Notre Dame.

IN THE TENS AND TWENTIES OF THIS CENTURY
all around Notre Dame were extensive farms
with rich soil and unusual productivity. They
were cared for by devoted Brothers. They
planted everything under the sun. There
were no better crops and no better meat for
our tables and food than that which came
from Brother Barnabas's gardens, Brother
Leo's cattle, and the produce of so many
trusty Brother workers at Saint Joseph Farm.
Picking strawberries, cherries, peas and beets
in all their picture-like and wholesome beauty
whetted our appetites, and made us grow
to pumpkin proportions. We feasted on the
famous Notre Dame buns in the morning and
on bread and cookies de luxe fashioned in
the best Holland tradition by Brothers who

were natives of Holland, and now operators of a neat bakery on our grounds. With milk from what were the best contented cows in the world, and meat from home-slaughtered cattle and sheep, cut and cured right on the spot, so to say, by one Belgian and one Pole, nothing was lacking, but nothing, to fill the eyes and the stomachs of dreaming boys. The farm chores we did outside of our class hours were excellent healthy exercises which contributed greatly to keep us trim and slim.

Saint Joseph's Farm nearest to Granger, Indiana, and not far from the University was its fairy provider. The Brother farmers, toned by their religious make-up and spirit, worked with an agricultural skill and finesse to turn out all produce, and alfalfa, barley, oats, wheat and corn to the admiration and perhaps some envy, on the part of their fellow enterprisers throughout the country fields. Prize cattle, and Blue Ribbon products, bespoke a deeply religious touch, and the summer and autumn sunshine displayed a wonderful harvest, failing, perhaps, only in an adequate Thanksgiving, that should be provided by men. But God, Himself, I am sure, was pleased and overjoyed at the efforts of our humble Brothers. "He crowned the year with his bounty, and your paths he overflowed with a rich harvest. Rejoicing clothed the hills, the fields were garmented with flocks, and the valleys with grain. We shouted and sang for joy." (Psalm LXIV:12, 13, 14). It is not too far-fetched to say that life at Notre Dame in those balmy and peaceful days was a summons to another Transfiguration of Our Lord for us to apply Saint Peter's eager sentiments: "Master, it is good for us to be here. Let us set up three tents" (Luke IX:33), one for the Priests, one for the Brothers and one for the Sisters,—and an extra one for us, unworthy Seminarians, and for all other people, always invited to Notre Dame, to taste its sweetness, and see what God was doing for us, who have vowed to love Him.

Of all the works done, the humblest and

the most necessary fell most of the time into the always most willing hands of the Brothers. There was among them a Brother Canute who did the menial jobs for his community. He moved about consistently with his "step and half gait," for he was a little lame. Like an angel in the infirmary, cheerful always, comforting and serving the sick, a welcomer and good wisher of a solid prayerful stock, he distinguished himself among those who love God. There was a Brother Leopold, the "Sweet Tooth of the University," from whom the students bought candy, and sometimes helped themselves freely without a charge. Was Brother missing it? He became suspicious, and he really and truly found out, when, as one of the students commented, he counted the jelly beans stored in a large bucket. Minor losses, however, were offset by the rapid sale of candy. The cookies and the lemonade too, marked by prominent student-proof numbers, were moving off the shelves under the old Brother's amiable and watchful supervision. Prayer and sacrifice kept things in perfect order as Brother Leopold and all the other Brothers acted like real dads of the students. One of them appeared completely broke. Wishing to send a telegram to his father, he came to one of the Brothers to borrow money. The good Brother gave him fifteen cents, just enough to send this bobtailed message: "No mon, no fun, your son!" It was the Brother's concoction for a student in dire distress. The answer came sooner than expected: "How sad, too bad, your dad." The Priests and the Brothers were always on the spot at the University to alleviate such "calamities," and life went on with hardly a semblance of a hitch.

The busiest corners at Notre Dame were to the right as you turned from the back lower entrance of the Main Building. There were the kitchen, "bee hives," where you were never stung. The Sisters of the Congregation of Holy Cross were the busy bees, immune to the students' "wise" remarks, and without any stingers. They were the cooks par excellence, honeyed to the ultimate quintessence of sweetness. Their names were too difficult to remember, so the students playfully renamed them as Sister Soup, Sister Steak, Sister Potato, Sister Gravy, Sister Salad, Sister Fruit, Sister Pie, Sister Ice Cream and Sister Coffee, according to what each of them made, handled and served. Sister Lourdes, as Sister Coffee, must have poured an ocean of it for the many years she served the students at Notre Dame in the atmosphere and grace like that of the Holy Shrine at Lourdes.

Helping the Sisters in everything was the most genial and friendly Irishman by the name of Jack Mangan, who came straight from the old sod. He not only handled cartons of food, but took upon himself to dig a ditch wherever needed, or to fix a roof, or crank and drive a car, or to sew a button on a jacket for any one, all these favors done with his broad smile. Jack was truly a "factotum," a gem of a charitable soul who turned thoroughly American for Notre Dame.

The best people at this sacred place put nationality prejudice aside. Human nature, no matter where it came from, was the same, so long as you realized what somebody had from Almighty God, and were willing to make the best of it. When these good people came across a boy, they all got together sympathetically and beautifully with help to see what they could make out of him. I allowed them to rear me. The Notre Dame Irish Americans had the stuff in them to build character and college upon a noble and promising French foundation and upon their own. Notre Dame was ultra cosmopolitan to me, promoting first and foremost the love of God and the love of one's neighbor. Here is where you were taught to mind your own business and never to hurt anybody. The broad-minded men and women of Irish descent gave this boy of Polish immigrants every chance in life that would have been given to any other boy. You were welcome at Notre Dame then, and I hope you are welcome now, as a cool breeze on a hot summer day, by the Priests, Brothers and Sisters who have constituted a true and solid American Catholic community, better known and acclaimed, justifiably so as "The Fightin' Irish."

Back to Jack Mangan who brought with him his brother Mike, who studied at Notre Dame, and made an excellent priest. Strong, zealous and always genial like Jack, he distinguished himself as a Holy Cross Missionary in far-off India, now Pakistan. God took him to heaven in his youthful years. The time he spent in mission work with his steady, sacrificing and profitable spirit is distinguished in the annals of the Holy Cross Congregation in India. I remember Mike most as a seminarian and my teammate in baseball, when he clobbered home runs. I often thought that Babe Ruth, Lou Gehrig and Mickey Mantle had done no better for the Yankees than Mike Mangan did for us. Jack Mangan outlived his brother for many years, and kept on being all things to all men, especially to the Priests and Brothers. There was never a more valuable layman at Notre Dame than Jack. Father John J. Cavenaugh, the President in Jack's time, appraised him highly. To show his appreciation he took Jack on a trip to see the championship game of the season between Notre Dame and Southern California. This was the last game.

Jack was decked out like the "Dude of the Dome." Suited anew to the tee, with a new tie and shoes for the first time professionally shined, he accompanied the players with an extra pep and big cheer. Coaching or playing was none of his business, but he looked no less dignified and important than any one on the squad. When the team arrived in Los Angeles, the newspaper man crowded around the Notre Dame personnel including Jack Mangan. He assumed an air of independence and silence, but stuck with the crowd. Everybody talked football without mentioning the football itself. Conversations ranged around signals, different formations, break-away plays, field goals, forward passes and touchdowns, tricky runs and such like maneuvers. Jack said not a word. He just listened and look smart. One of the newshawks who was eyeing him often and surreptitiously, whispered into Father Cavenaugh's ear: "Who is the man in the dark suit?" Father Cavenaugh, anticipating this situation, answered quickly with playful surity: "He is the team's chief strategist." More than satisfied with this information, the anxious reporter of a leading paper, thinking he had an exclusive scoop, and expecting a volume of stratagems, edged his way politely but cautiously to the side of the master of secret craft on the coaching staff of Notre Dame, and surprised Jack Mangan with this question: "Sir, what are you going to use tomorrow?" Suspicious of some sporty introduction of himself, and looking at Father Cavenaugh's dancing eyes, Jack was quick to catch on to the jocose strategy, and with all his Irish hidden humor shot the query right back into the face of the avid newshound: "What are we going to use tomorrow? What? A football." That was all of it for the disappointed newsman. He declared Jack's clever response as a master stroke in strategy, and went off even without saying "Thank you." Father Cavenaugh and I have long since nominated Jack Mangan for the Hall of Fame as the All American, all time *strategist*, who remembered that the first thing to be used in a Football Game is *a football*.

AT THE DOORWAY OF MY CASTLE OF DREAMS was an outstanding *alter christus* or *another Christ*, as a priest should be. He was Thomas

Patrick Irving, truly a noble soul. When you shook his hand, you felt two hearts, one his own and the other Christ's. To his fatherly love and care I attribute my youthful career at Notre Dame. I fell into Father Irving's arms on my first day, and I parted with him close to his dying day in his eighty-seventh year. I declare him now as the All American and All Heaven Trainer of Priests. He was like a book written on Christ, open for you, so you could read always something with relish, something more perfect. He knew how to deal with boys, especially the slightly spoiled ones. He was magnanimous and magnificent in sorting out candidates for Christ. In a conference one day, he made it crystal clear to us that it was no one else but Christ who brought us to Notre Dame. You may be not yet right or ripe for Him, but you are still holding His hand, he said. That all depends on you. Just look into His face, and ask Him to help you keep the rules of this seminary. They are His blessed rules which can make one altogether fit for Him in His sacred priesthood. Obey, and you will get grace from Him, sufficient to solve all your doubts and fears—sufficient to overcome your lassitude and indifference. Note this, no matter what vocation you choose, you may never in your life turn away from Christ. Father Irving was giving us nothing greater than the first and last word on Who Christ was, Who He is, and Who He will always be. This was Father Irving's way, on an even keel in his reasoning and simple philosophy. He gave me the true idea of a vocation, and I fell in love with it. Unworthy of Christ's grace, I followed His call.

Father Irving could take a joke as well as the rest of us. This one was on him, played by me at the instigation of a dear friend of his, Father Joseph Burke, who himself, was an ace in the priesthood at Notre Dame. When the nifty golf course replaced the farms in front of the University, enthusiasm for that sport ran high everywhere, so much so that it even grabbed Father Irving. In his room you would have found a set of clubs and a number of golf balls. I had charge of his rooms, but I was not his caddy. One evening during Father Irving's absence, in came Father Joe and spotted the golf balls scattered somewhat in the corner of the room. Father Burke, always ready for some innocent mischief, suggested to me: "Tell you what you do. When you make up Father Irving's bed for tonight, take a few of these balls and put them in between the sheets at the foot of his bed. They will keep nice and snug and cool there. When Father gets in there and touches those balls with his toes, he will jump out like nobody's business, thinking that mice are running all over his feet." It worked just that way. I hated to do this to my superior, even if I could share the blame with Father Joe. Woe betide me the next morning. I reported sheepishly to my job. Father Irving looked very serious, and acted as if he were somehow hurt. I broke the silence by telling him first that there was a visitor in his room last night. He guessed immediately who the joker was, and when I confessed my part in the conspiracy, he forgave me with a promise to get even and doubly so with Father Joe: "If he had only seen me last night, leaping out of my bed post haste, he would have swallowed his Adam's apple from laughter, and kept rolling like those golf balls all over the floor."

One day I suddenly fell ill. Dressed in my best suit, collar and tie, I threw myself on my bed in the dormitory. The boys spread the alarm, and Father Irving came quickly to see me. He diagnosed my case, I guess, as a little gas on my stomach, and his remedy was this remark to my pals around me: "Look at Jan, he's all dressed up, and has no place to go. He's ready to turn up his toes to the daisies, and that's the end of Jan." With a twinkle in his eye he placed his hands with a press on my head and blessed me. I flipped feet first out of my bed with no sign of sickness whatsoever. When I am ready to pass away, I hope the thought of Father Irving drifts through my mind. It will be easier for me to die. Among all his perfections God, to be sure, counts a sense of humor, for that is a perfection, and Father Irving had it in abundance from God.

IT WILL NOT BE AMISS TO MENTION AT LEAST one of the seminarians, who among my other fellows was pleasant and wonderful to live with. He was Donald MacGregor, a Scotchman from Canada. His feet were larger than an average man's, but he would say they were large enough to give you a solid foundation on the ground. His naive heart in size measured well up to one of them. Always neutral, he was a professed argument settler. With his amusing traits and Scottish peculiarities he was cut out to be an interesting and attractive clergyman. An average student, he posed as quite a versifier who without any warning could turn bits of conversation into screaming and sometimes caustic rhymes. He was a poet of sorts, who vied with the rest of them on the pages of the Scholastic, the Notre Dame Student Weekly. He could take more ribbing than anybody else without flying off his Scottish balance. Strong, built for hard labor, he was assigned the job of the steam man in the seminary. This required him to get up much earlier than we did in the morning to get the house warm. Being a sound sleeper, he put his faith in what he thought was a trusty old alarm clock. It failed him now and then, so Don went to Father Irving with his old, rusty grievance, no longer fit for regularity. The kind superior decided on a brand-new alarm clock for Don MacGregor. He was sent to town to be the purchaser. But poor Don was far from being up-to-date on alarm clocks. When he came to the store, and the clerk showed him the latest alarm clock, guaranteed to run for eight days after one full winding, Don was mystified, puzzled and dumbfounded. He never heard of such a thing. Was it possible? Yes, the clerk said this timepiece would tick eight days on the right dot, and ring any time you want it to, if you wind it and set it to suit yourself. Eight days from this hour, the clerk insisted. This was something beyond the credence of a Scot. This phenomenon was worth the trial. The clerk wound a brand-new alarm clock, and MacGregor closed the deal. Jubilant, but still skeptical, he brought it to his room for the crucial and convincing test. Then he began bragging all in detail about the clock in the recreation room before his confrères. One of them, quick to sense a funny idea, aimed to egg Don on to increase his faith in his alarm clock, and to score a hit on the Scotchman's innocence. As long as the timepiece was under Don's careful scrutiny, it would run out in eight days. Without his knowing it, why not keep winding it every day from now on. That was simple, as long as the mystical clock-winder could sneak into Don's room, when he was not there. The mischief worked, known to everybody except Don. The clock kept on ticking even after eight full days. Wonder of wonders! Puzzled at this, Don shook the clock furiously to get some kind of explanation, but it just splendidly ticked on. His Scottish mind failed to solve the mystery, so Don decided to go back with the alarm clock to the clerk to pay for it, and at the same time question his underestimation of this timepiece, still running very smoothly way beyond eight days, after what Don thought was its original winding. Not until he returned home with the clock under his arm was the mystery solved for him. The culprit "spilled the beans" amid a volley of laughter in the recreation room. To fool Mac-Gregor was to put a golden notch in your character. This time it was Frank Butler, later one of our best Fathers, who did it. But MacGregor, like the good sport he always was, took it in stride, joined all of us in the alarm clock jubilee, and wondered with gratitude at the things God wrought for him.

I must not forget that Don too was a cornet player of some note, and not altogether of a sour note either. He sneaked up often on his own musical scores to blow tunes from "Roamin in the Gloamin" to "Yankee Doodle Dandy," if not to please, at least to tease the listeners. After his ordination he took his beloved cornet along to the Holy Cross Missions in India. He prayed, preached and played there for every bit of forty years. In his leisure hours you could see him seated in front of his mission hut serenading the moon far into the night. One of his fellow missioners noticed that whenever MacGregor played his cornet, the moon would frown and change phases way ahead of her scheduled time. This, of course, was only a fanciful observation to belittle Don's moonlight concerts. From first to last he stuck to his cornet like the Hindus stuck to their caste. When he came back to the States his hallowed instrument nestled like a living chum under his arm. While he was still a seminarian, I penned these lines to Don:

Stand, Don MacGregor, stand behind your
  cornet and blow
Till that ornery trumpet of yours will swell
  and grow
And grow, as big as a sousaphone, to change
  its monotone.
Bravo, a Scotchman, you will really have to
  toot
And blast away a bass; but sorry, not in a
  kiltie suit.

In 1960 Don MacGregor wrote: "Since I have passed by two and a half years the time alotted to men here below, I thought it smart to pen my epitaph, before it is too late. I don't believe in leaving to others what I can do for myself. And then, too, I don't know what others might say. Here it is:

"Beneath this stone lies quite alone
The dust of Donald Mac;
Don't wait for him, though eyes be dim,
He'll not be coming back.
But, if you care, just say a prayer
For yours and his salvation,
That once for all, you may forestall
Both yours and his damnation."

Father Donald P. MacGregor died in 1967, ever buoyant and dear to all hearts, this Scotch-American. May his soul and all the souls of our faithful departed rest in peace. Amen.

I AM GOING BACK FOR A LITTLE WHILE YET TO
our Brothers. I have ever loved their vocation, their zeal and their skill. There were
Brothers around the grounds and barns,
where horses, mules, cows and steers were
tethered. You could see faithful Brother
Hugh. You could not miss him. He was big
and round, with the cognomen of "Huge."
He would not take any guff from anybody.
When you minded your own business, you
were Brother Hugh's, Huge's or Huie's best
friend. He went from field to field and from
barn to barn as an ace overseer and trouble-
shooter. Part of his time he devoted to instructing men who needed to be put on the
straight and narrow path. Strangers, odd
characters, were attracted to Notre Dame.

Brother Hugh did not invite them but he welcomed many a vagrant, hobo or down-and-outer who straggled into the grounds. He had a process of rehabilitation all his own, and in most cases it really worked.

Take for example one man whom we called Angelo. Brother Hugh made him work in and around the stables, and drive the horses hitched to large utility wagons. Angelo was a confirmed drunkard. He worked between his often broken promises and Brother's heroic tolerance. While under the influence of liquor, he fell asleep in a barn, and was kicked by a mule. Brother did not give up on Angelo. He saw to it that his broken leg was set and healed. Angelo, however, had to hobble around with a limp for the rest of his life. He was a stubby cheerful little man with a big head and a broad smile which truly stretched from ear to ear. Just to look at him would put you in the throes of uncontrollable laughter. Besides his propensity to alcoholic sprees, he was given to spitfire-cursing in the Polish

Two Notre Dame All-Time Greats:
Knute Rockne and George Herman Gipp

language, for he was a Polish-American. I was instrumental in breaking him of this habit. Here is how it happened. We, as seminarians, were hired for a very cheap wage to move the old, old library from the Main Building. The job was done by relaying the books in succession on to our friend Angelo's big wagon. He was driving us and the horses to and from the building, preceding the newest library. This structure has been since given over to the Architectural students. It was built and dedicated in Notre Dame's Diamond Jubilee year, 1917.

Late, on one of the library-moving afternoons Angelo, seeming very tired after the day's work, completely lost his patience. He began accusing us bitterly in broken English of laying down on the job and cursing like a trooper in excellent, but damnable Polish, which he knew much better than any other language. And here is where I chimed in to remonstrate against his foul speech in my best Polish. This was a complete check on him, and he was so surprised he nearly fell off the wagon. He never suspected that one of us matched his nationality. So the two Poles, he and I, got acquainted for the first time, and the fire of his invective vanished forever with its smoke. Never did I see a man more repentant and so apologetic, promising with all his heart never to curse again. I think Angelo, a friend now of all of us boys and of everybody from this happening on, never again used a bad word in his life.

But to his number one weakness, Angelo, if I recall rightly, returned only once. He got drunk. The occasion was Armistice Day in 1918. We found him on one of those memorable, mutual admiration street cars running from South Bend to Notre Dame. Seated in it rather restlessly, after his celebration of this historical day, was the inebriated Angelo opposite me. Right next to him sat Father Matthew Walsh, once the President of Notre Dame, a fine, finished religious gentleman and a thoroughly sympathetic priest. Father

Walsh who knew Angelo very well, was giving some attention to his incoherent prattling and gesticulating manner of this alcoholic good feeler. Father Walsh interrupted: "Angelo, what makes you drink so much?", and Angelo, who was ever courteous to a priest, answered: "Nothing, Father, I just volunteer." Father Walsh continued: "Did you ever take the pledge, Angelo?" "The pledge, yes I did, Father, many times, but I ain't started keeping it yet." That threw the whole car into a merry uproar which may have touched Angelo's heart in the right spot, for I had heard that shortly after he got off at Notre Dame, he did renew his pledge, and started to keep it in earnest for good. He turned out to be an honest working man all along for quite a few years, and died a peaceful and happy death. Angelo was but one of the many lost sheep whom Brother Hugh brought back to the fold. The good Brother, gruff in his manner at times, walked with his rosary in his hand to the crypt of Sacred Heart Church as gently as a dove of

peace, to beg for strength to handle recalci-
trant tramps and bring them hope, shelter
and salvation.

What puzzled me in those blessed days
was that Brother Hugh purchased a good-
sized mule, a real jackass with the biggest
ears I have ever seen on such an animal. He
kept him working and braying on the farm
facing Notre Dame, and the noise which the
huge animal made, hardly harmonized with
the peal of the gentle bells and chimes in the
tower of the church. His lungs labored like
a steaming caliope to broadcast for miles
around. One student who ironically called
this mule the "Campus Canary," offered to
be his skinner to drive him away from Notre
Dame to nowhere. I think that Brother Hugh
himself got the biggest kick out of this
"Campus Canary," and kept him purposely,
not so much for work as for an example to all
of us that "jackasses" of the human kind were
never to be welcomed or tolerated at Notre
Dame.

In summer Brother Hugh spent many a

day at Bankson Lake, Lawton, Michigan where our vacation camp was located. It too prospered under his devoted care. The folks in that vicinity regarded and respected him as the jolly gentleman farmer from Notre Dame. He was to them good Sunday company. Many of them did not know that he was a religious Brother, and invited him to bring his wife and children along. Brother Hugh would pass this courtesy off with a wink to his Brother companion without saying "Yes" or "No," for he liked to keep some things secret. What was God's belonged to God with him. I have long placed Brother Hugh in the Hall of Fame at Notre Dame, the All American and the All Time "Rehabilitator" of men.

Speaking of Bankson Lake, I will allow briefly another Brother to enter the picture. He was the bushy white-haired old Cajetan. He was in charge of the smallest students, who lived in Saint Edward's Hall, and some of whom acquired the name of "Lifers," because they stayed at Notre Dame through all the years to become seniors, graduates and alumni. In summer most of these boys came to camp. There were no livelier, smarter and more mischievous kids in the whole world. The more devilry they perpetrated on us adult campers, the happier they were. It was fun for them to put slimy bull frogs between the sheets in our beds, when we were not there, and resort to other trickery at our expense. We depended on the angelic white shepherd, Brother Cajetan, with his strong cane to hold them in reasonable check. These presumably innocent lambkins were taught in Saint Edward's Hall by the Sisters of Holy Cross. When the classes were in session in the afternoon, Brother would seek relief from the ordinary juvenile tumult by betaking himself to the hall chapel. But even then and there, the house cat followed him in. Brother ordered him to lie down and keep still. At the fourth station the pet feline was again at Cajetan's feet, meouing. Brother picked him up, tucked him under his arm, and continued making his Way of the Cross with an accompaniment of hushes and meous. I admired Brother Cajetan for his candid simplicity in all that he did, because behind it all was his loving solicitude portraying a White Shepherd. With a sincere love of God for men, women and children and even for pets, he was leading with his trusty cane ranks upon ranks of little boys to the classroom, chapel and playfield to make them grow into excellent Notre Dame men and valuable citizens of their country.

NEXT FROM MY DREAMLAND, STEPPING INTO singular and emphatic reality, was a precisely idealistic man, Knute Rockne. His University and his universal acclaim are inseparable. This does not mean that Notre Dame was necessarily built on this "Rock." Long before Rockne appeared as a promising young student, Notre Dame, spurred and guided by the love of God and His Blessed Mother, was well on its way to a beautiful and remarkable recognition and success. The long voyage of Father Sorin and his companions from France to what still was Indian wilderness, dotted with two refreshing lakes, was ever recalled to strengthen the spirit of those who continued their work. The pioneering Fathers and Brothers with the encouraging help of the prayerful Sisters, all ultra-religious souls, who by their stand-in with the Immaculate Mother of God, their hopes and sacrifices, hard labor and hardships, established a solid Rock of Spirituality, which should never be weakened, compromised or surrendered. The wonderful people who came after them put their genius willingly to work always upon this Rock of Spirituality, always in view of the Lady on the Dome, to manufacture, as it

Stadium, University of Notre Dame

were, their dreams into a wholesome reality.

Heaven-sent Rockne, who upheld all these builders of Notre Dame, was a *layman,* a character, destined to fire a giant impetus for his Alma Mater. His was a strong and nifty physique, blessed with a dynamic personality. First of all we must not forget his academic stature. In his studies he towered head and shoulders over most of the other students, especially in chemistry, and became a proficient instructor in that department under the guidance of our Father Julius Nieuwland, the All-American scientist. But Rockne's heart belonged with athletics. He tried everything in sports, even pole vaulting. In this field event, as in all he practiced for, he aimed high, but he fell short of breaking any records except in football. He saved his agility, ability and prowess for that sport. He had an uncanny way of figuring, inventing and exposing all possible intricacies of this game. He handled and tossed, he blocked and tackled, he kicked and caught the football with phenomenal skill to train his players. With almost unbelievable succession they won the games for Notre Dame. They aroused the football world to utmost admiration and imitation. Men, women and children wondered, and were asking what was there at Notre Dame that brought youthful men of such calibre, and outfitted them to study, pray and play as nobody had done before.

Rockne, himself a player, captained the team to victory over the Army at West Point in 1913. Saturday, November 1st of that year, has been well remembered and will be referred to on and on as the day on which Notre Dame trimmed probably the most touted team in the nation 35 to 13. The welcome news came to us by way of a telegram, and from then on, Rockne and his teammates began to scale the heights of heroism, as far as the students were concerned. The celebration they staged for this victory portended an era of interesting football at Notre Dame with an acute desire and struggle for championship year after year. *"Cheer, cheer for old Notre Dame"* never sounded louder or better. Its echoes were drowned out by ringing bells, blowing horns and drumming drums. The horses from the neighboring farms added their neighing, the sheep their bleating, and everybody their singing, to beat the band. This made the cheering completely de luxe, like a grand rehearsal for all the victories to come.

Notre Dame began collecting a fabulous fandom from coast to coast and from all over the world where American football was known and appreciated. The Vatican harbored the most famous Number One Fan, His Holiness Pius XII. He was interested enough to try and foretell months ahead of time the outcome of a forthcoming game between Notre Dame and Army to a contingent of American soldiers, enjoying an audience with him. The Holy Pontiff said that Notre Dame would win by a big score. This pitched the G.I.'s to such a height of enthusiasm that one of them was willing to bet a considerable amount of money on Notre Dame. He believed in papal infallibility. But here he did not know that he was making an entirely wrong application. Thinking that he was right in his decision, he staked his money right and left on Notre Dame and his faith absolutely on the Holy Father's friendly prediction. Secretly he gloried in what he thought was a cinch for him. When the football season got under way and the Notre Dame-Army game was played with its outcome papally foretold, it turned out to be just the opposite of what the Holy Father had said. The Army, and not Notre Dame, won the game by a big score, and the poor soldier lost his money. How could that be? Infallibility failed. He almost lost his faith. Sorry, soldier, but you have to study your religion a little more. Papal infallibility does not enter into the oval of football, even if it were as wide as all the stadia in the world. The Holy Father simply took a guess as any fan would, and sadly missed. The soldier understood. He lost his money, but not his faith.

The best player to catch anybody's eye, whom Rockne sized up well for football, was George Herman Gipp. From a physical point of view he had a perfect form for the grid-iron, and socially, you could not find a man with a bigger heart for you and Notre Dame. I considered it a mighty privilege to have been seated next to him in one of my classes. Here was my opportunity to pick up a great deal of information about the mental attitude of our athletes, their hard work in practice, and their love for the sympathetic and in-domitable Rockne. Gipp and I exchanged our views on football topics, when we took advantage of the professor's breaks in our history of philosophy class. Gipp supplied me with a lot of football data, and I tried to help him a little in philosophy. In return I got more from him than simply talk. My reward was the satisfaction of seeing him, my hero, in all the games, take the football from center, and run all the way for touchdowns, power his way over the opponents' line or eluding his opponents. With his brawny outstretched arms, he was beautiful to behold: he embraced the football, passed to him to the end zone, as he scooted for a rousing six-pointer for Notre Dame. When things were going tough and rough for his team, I saw him punt far out of danger, or uncork a forward pass, as easily as blowing a bubble, to a receiver, free at the opponents' goal line. In all my exuberance I imagined the football was thrown to me. Gipp was an expert punter, and he could heave that pigskin far and accurately out of the opposing players' reach, but, I thought, never out of my grip, for usually on Monday mornings an imaginary football tossed by Gipp nestled close to my heart. I congratulated him on his prowess which was a thing of beauty for me and all the Notre Dame fans. It took Knute Rockne, the master coach, to spot the master player, George Gipp, to produce the *master stroke*

in football, winning games for Notre Dame.
Other coaches came and went, players followed upon players, but when it came to buck
up against odds for the team, the thought
of the *"The Rocker"* and the "Gipper" was
enough to supply that extra push for the winning touchdown. George Gipp died *when
football was in flower, and he in his college
togs. He was in the Knighthood of his career,
just in time to win the favor of his conversion
to the faith, and become forever the hero of
the Lady of the Dome.*

For his own amusement Rockne indulged
at the expense of his lads in what may be
called a heart play in football. He was out to
make men out of them. A student who was
turning out to be just a mediocre player fitted
himself out for football and Rockne had him
on the roster for every game. He grew very
fond of this fellow, in as much as what he
lacked in playing ability, he made up with
his cheerfulness and a novel way of boosting
the team's morale. Rockne let him play now

111

and then but most of the time he kept him on the sidelines. "Rock, when do I go in?" was his usual question, and Rockne's answer followed quickly, calmly and repeatedly: "I am saving you." In his last year on the team, when time was already running out on this senior, the very last game of the season being played, this lad, usually warming the bench, leaped up towards Rockne, lost his patience and blurted out in a commanding tone: "For heaven's sake, when do I go in?" Rockne was unperturbed, and in a gentle and courteous expression responded in the self same way: "I am saving you!" Then came the explosion: "What in the hell are you saving me for, Rock?" and the coach served up to him as if on a platter this final reply: "I have saved you for the senior ball." It may have hurt the boy, but he did not show it. The football season ended right then and there, and Rockne proved that he was a heart player as well as a football player. In the locker room he called aside this all American team morale booster and candidate for the senior ball, and with an apologetic justification for his playful football circumstance he congratulated him on his efforts, emphasizing particularly his fine spirit of geniality, encouragement and cooperation. The two, coach and player, parted the best of friends. The young monogrammed alumnus may have well said to Rockne: "In all your different humors, whether grave or lightsome, you are such a pungent yet tasty and pleasant hunk of humanity that I could carry you on my shoulders single-handed all around the Notre Dame Stadium." Rockne may have well responded: "You have enough spleen and guts in you, and so much wit and spunk that there is no living without you, so I make you one of my assistants."

Rockne's teams had their signals barked out by the quarterback immediately before each play. All plans and all strategy had to be in their skulls. When the players huddled, it was more for a moment of prayer, usually for a Hail Mary or two or three. Rockne was a believer in prayer. This was Notre Dame's most important signal. The opponents caught on, perhaps not altogether, but enough to be interested. They decided on the same tactic. The Army captain assured his coach that before the next game with the Irish he would pray with his teammates in the huddle. The coach most heartily approved. When the game came off, sure enough, in their huddle before each play they prayed and prayed like monks, but the Notre Dame boys outprayed and outplayed them, and came near to swamping them. After the game the down-hearted squad came straggling off the Yankee Stadium with sobs and tears. The Army coach muffled the scene just to rub it in: "Well, did you fellows really pray?" The captain was first to answer: "Yes, coach, we did pray. We prayed like hell, but we could not catch them." That was the way of the Notre Dame squad. Speed, faith, spirit and courage plus a few Hail Marys beat practically all opponents. How about the few losses? The players took them all in stride like good sports just as did their humble ace, Knute Rockne. Father Irving, who always knew how to take a defeat with a stout heart, and I, who took it hard, saw Rock going across the campus on the Monday after the Saturday, October 8th, 1921, when Notre Dame was beaten by Iowa 10 to 7. Father Irving shouted at some distance: "Good morning, Rock, what seemed to be the matter there in Iowa?" Rockne's wide smile returned the greeting to us, and then he added: "Thought they were All Americans," meaning, of course, our boys. He kept on walking, leaving it to us to figure out why his team came home on the short end of the score. Father Irving and I arrived at the same conclusion: "Smile on, Rock, the next Saturday you will win," and win he did.

When Knute Rockne met his tragic death on March 31, 1931 in an aeroplane accident at Bazaar, Kansas, I lost a dear friend. In my grief I lost also all my love for air travel.

Since then, I have been sticking closely to the words in the Holy Bible: "Man is born to labor and the *bird* to fly." It was sudden, shocking and stunning to millions of Notre Dame fans to hear of Rockne's death. He would be no longer on the football field, and no longer with us. His untimely demise was the departure of his sincere soul at the peak of his popularity and honor. For us it created a continuous sadness, for him eternal joy.

On that gloomy day I felt like the newspaper boy on one of the streets of a Southern town, before whose eyes flashed the headline *"Rockne Killed."* The little fellow threw his bundle of papers on the ground, and falling on his hands and knees, peered over the big letters, "ROCKNE KILLED," and began shedding Niagara Falls in miniature. How many tears streamed down the cheeks of this boy and all the people at large nobody will ever tell, but the most consoling comfort in this tragedy was to learn of Rockne's rosary, wound firmly around his hand, and found immediately upon the discovery of his body. He evidently called the best signal in time for his short and quick journey to the final goal. He won the greatest victory for himself and Notre Dame. From the poor newsboy on the street to the noblest of the Notre Dame fans, Pope Pius XII, people pooled their prolific prayers into something like a huge make-believe FOOTBALL to pass it forward to Rockne, so he might catch it like he did the real football, and run to score his last touch-down in the eternal Zone of Heaven.

By most sportsmen and football lovers Rockne was voted the *Best Coach in the Hundred Years of Football.*

✤   ✤   ✤

Father Charles L. O'Donnell was the President of Notre Dame when Rockne passed away. He delivered a scholarly eulogy at the funeral. No one could have done better, for the souls of Rockne, Father O'Donnell and that of the Founder Father Sorin were closely knit together in talent, desire and effort for a greater Notre Dame. To remind us of Father Sorin we love these lines written by Father O'Donnell:

Founder's Day

This is the tree, whose root he set
That bitter spring, in stubborn soil;
God's sunny grace and man's hard toil
Have reared it thus, nor fail it yet.

A tree of many branches now
It towers among time's mighty ones,
The mothering home of many sons,
The fruit of Sorin's triple vow.

Thoughts like these born in Father O'Donnell's mind and heart feed the flame of Father Sorin's blessed torch for light, guidance and life. It was one of my happy graces to have Father O'Donnell as a teacher in English. Into our classroom one day, he invited his fellow-poet, Joyce Kilmer, the author of "Trees," the poem quoted a few pages back. He himself recited his immortal line with a commanding artistic touch. He was a mild-mannered man whose beady eyes betrayed a wealth of inspiring thoughts, and also a definite spark of courage, ennabling him later in life to give up his life for his country in World War I. With all the pride I had, and utmost courtesy I put my hand in his. Somehow I was forming a resolution to uphold this man, Joyce Kilmer, to all our American youth as one of our greatest fathers, poets, soldiers and heroes.

TO POINT TO THE STRAIGHT AND NARROW PATH, and set the world right, there is a constant call for serious thinkers, philosophers, who must apply their reasoning powers first and foremost to the concept of God in order to arrive absolutely and unequivocally at the truth that cannot be changed or divided. A philosopher, to be genuine, must employ none other than the time-honored and right rules in searching for knowledge, beginning with our easily recognizable, and even felt, indisputable relationship with the Triune God. Once having discovered the Truth in its entirety, as limited to man, it becomes the philosopher's duty to accept truth wholeheartedly, unconditionally and joyfully, and to pass it on pure and unadulterated to all mankind.

Such a philosopher, who most ably answered the call, I knew, and I saw blossom into one of Notre Dame's best teachers. I have Father Charles Miltner in mind. Truth, I have learned from him at the very outset, is the greatest word in any language, for truth is like unto God, and very often used as His cognomen. When we say God, we also mean Christ, for Christ was God from all eternity, and even as a Man on earth, He was God; is God *now*, and ever will be God. His Father in Heaven made it plain that His only begotten Son must be listened to and obeyed.

When Pilate, that ignominious judge, faced Christ, he was ignorant of what truth meant. He did not know that the prisoner before him was truth itself. However, the haughty Roman got curious enough to ask: "What is truth?" Christ for the moment ignored him, because with his calloused and unjust mind the pagan deserved no answer. Furthermore Christ chose to keep silence in the presence of the bloodthirsty rabble. Any defense of the truth by Jesus or anybody else in that illegal trial would have incited the mob to hurl a volley of contradiction, scorn and derision, dishonor and insult on the Son of God. One person, a member of the Sanhedrin, could have dared to rise in protest, but this disciple of Christ like the rest of them, kept his mouth shut. Gamaliel was the name of this friend of Christ, and he was the only one among those crooked judges in the Sanhedrin or the Council of the Jews. Because of his lack of courage, he did not say a word in defense of Christ to vindicate Him before the crafty Annas, his assistant Caiphas, and Pilate.

Today Christ is on trial again, but not as He was before Pilate of old. He was there visible, in person. But now Christ is absent. He is at the bar of human judgement under a sort of a man-conceived subterfuge to save the face of the falsely-judicial thinkers and philosophers, who by their subtle and spurious arguments twist the words of Christ from their right meaning in the Gospels, and cleverly blot out the truth. But do not worry, these philosophers, and I may add, theologians, are approaching a legion in numbers. If they do not turn about soon, they will be facing some day a "crucifixion" of their own. We shall all die, and Christ and no one else will be our judge. He was the One, Who said: "Heaven and earth shall pass away, but my words shall not pass away."

Christ, who was totally abandoned at the infamous trial in Jerusalem, as He stood before Pilate from whom he evoked the words *ecce homo* at the sight of His precious blood, today stands invisibly glorious, risen and triumphant, *ecce rex regum*, "behold the king of kings." Always and everywhere Christ must be known, honored, loved and defended, as ever, the total, and, the totally unchangeable truth. I regret that Father Miltner is no longer alive. He would surely be a minuteman for the defense of truth. He would stand up bright and right against the modern philosophical and theological foolishness spreading all over the world, and tainting Notre Dame. With all the powers of his soul he would challenge the hide-and-seek testimony against the words of Christ, and he would put to shame the perverters of truth, and scandalmongers rising even from the fold of the Holy Church. There are some who have been secretly, if not openly, shaking their fists at Christ. They defy rightly constituted authority by using strange and futile arguments against the One, Holy, True, Apostolic and Universal Church, sidetracking her precepts, shirking the Ten Commandments, and wrongfully interpreting Christ's blessed words on truth, justice and peace. They simply ignore what is the surest way to eternal life in Heaven: poverty, chastity and obedience. They are the *Modern Rabble,* who, it seems by devil-thought-up innovations, allow *Religion* and *Conduct* to split way apart, and cause men, women and children to drift along promiscuously into the continuous swirl of pride, turbulence and crime.

16

PRIESTS WHO DEFECT FROM THE TRUTH, THE Way and the Life have taken the proper study of Christ very lightly, and this is one of the important reasons why they have left the Church. They soon become a band of ruthless religious *pirates,* who prey upon the hearts of the people, and knowing that they cannot destroy Grace itself, they work in co-operation with the evil spirit to deflect it by shameless scandal. They try to sacrifice their priesthood on the altar of the demon, and according to Saint Jude, they are ungodly men who turn the grace of God into wantonness and disown our only Master and Lord, Jesus Christ. These "men love darkness rather than light, because their deeds are evil." (John III:19). What should have been solid virtue between them and their MASTER has been superseded by crass intellectual pride, very often politely called intellectual freedom. Intellectual pride is an ugly sin. It was first conceived in Heaven by Lucifer and his cohorts. At the instant of their guilt, they were changed into evil spirits, cut down by the flaming sword of Saint Michael, the Archangel, and plunged into the deep abyss of hell. Subject to the same divine justice and condemnation are all dissenters from the truth of Christ, the Word, God-Man and Our Saviour. At the time, when intellectual pride began to exercise its wickedness, and Lucifer prevailed upon Adam and Eve, Our Heavenly Father in His infinite mercy introduced His Only Begotten Son and His Virgin Mother: "I will place enmity between you and the woman, between your seed and her seed; he shall crush your head, and you shall lie in wait for her heel." (Genesis III:15). From then on, it became the binding duty of every human being to fight phony philosophy and questionable theology to prevent their mode of reasoning from casting shadow and error upon the image of Christ and upon His words. What right has anyone to obliterate the alpha and omega which must dominate all human endeavor? How dare anyone discredit the Epistles of Saint Paul or the Works of Saint Thomas or Saint Augustine and the other Doctors of the Church, who were the first, and are still the time-honored interpreters of Christ's words in the Holy Gospels? Moreover who can with a clear conscience pass by or sweep off altogether from library shelves such a book as the "Imitation of Christ" by Thomas a Kempis, a masterpiece of thought and meditation for truth-loving souls?

Father Miltner was a humble priest, thoroughly devoted to his vocation; a philosopher of the first rank, and a loving disciple of Christ. We need men like him *today*. You could see him standing, and only standing for long hours at his specially made high desk to keep himself always awake, while he kept thumping and thumping on the keys of his typewriter his power-thoughts for pure, unadulterated *truth*. He was standing, as I have said, because for him, it was not just right and proper at all to sit and fall asleep on the job for Almighty God.

Do you know that the evil spirit, commonly known as the devil, the past master of all unbelief and the father of lies, can by permission of Almighty God cover himself with a false image of Jesus Christ? Pretending to be the real saviour carrying His Cross, the demon makes the resemblance so perfect that an ordinary human being will find it very hard to catch on to his trick.

Like a "lion he lurks seeking whom he may devour." In his maliciously designed trap, he couches his infamous lips behind what really looks like the all sympathetic and all beautiful face of Christ to spew forth with his ignominious tongue opinions contrary to the truth in the Holy Gospel itself. He begins, perseveres, and often succeeds with this, his most powerful temptation, to baffle priests and religious.

Is there any one to help you then? Do you know what will be the best thing for you to do, if you, perchance, should be confronted by this deplorable baiting of your soul? If you have your faith right handy and steadfast, you will immediately turn your mind and heart to "Our fallen nature's solitary boast," the Blessed Virgin Mary, who is ever aware of the most insidious schemes of the devil. She is the only one who can immediately detect the evil spirit faking Christ. She, who crushed the serpent's head, will instantly uncover the masquerader, if you will quickly call upon her to come to your aid.

A dear and honest thought of her will shoo the devil away. She knows and loves her Divine Son too well to be fooled by any disguise of Him. For she is by far the greatest "Go Between" between you and God, her Divine Son. With your heart close to hers you are safe, because her mantle of Divine Grace covers you. Greet her with a "Hail Mary," and you will feel the demon running away post haste to his bottomless hell. You will at once become aware that no doubt, no indifference, no amount of argument, and no defection whatsoever on your part can in any way blot out the sacred meaning, significance and importance of Divine Grace, as through Mary it rests forever, shining at the pinnacle of the Holy Priesthood and the Holy Mass to adore the true image of Christ. Be watchful, be sober, resist all temptations, you, steadfast in your faith. (Peter V:5).

Time has come when according to Saint Paul men and women do *not now* listen to sound teaching, but with ears itching, pile for themselves teachers to suit their pleasure. They turn hearing away from truth to fables. If you are a fallen priest, perhaps, you cannot exactly be classed with such notorious characters as "Billy, The Kid," but what that man once said, you can well repeat many times for yourself: "I am headed straight for Hell, and I am taking with me as many as I can." So there is no time like the present to *turn about face, back to Jesus Christ, who lives and reigns on earth as well as in heaven forever.*

Thank God we have priests, Brothers and Sisters who keep to the straight and narrow path, the way of the truth. All Heaven bless them for holding on to the truth with all their hearts and minds—upholding it and thereby showing good example to the young and the old laymen and women, and especially to the children. The genuine Religious have, as it were, a remarkable sixth sense, which immediately experiences and registers caution, detects the evil spirit, and summons courage and stability to increase their love and the service of God.

Our present Holy Father, Pope Paul VI, had these good shepherds in mind when he recently called our attention to them:

"We want to comfort the vocation of these

generous and courageous souls franchised from the world in which paradoxically they go on living in order to seek in the fulness of love, CHRIST,—the brothers and sisters and the world itself in the humbleness of service and in the greatness of sacrifice." *Revere and love them. They pray for you unceasingly.*

Let us humbly bow our heads before Christ and take in His words: "I have come a light to the world, that whoever believes in me may not remain in darkness. And if anyone hears my words, and does not keep them, it is not I who judge him, for I have not come to judge the world, but to save the world. He who rejects me, and does not accept my words has one to condemn him on the last day. For I have not spoken on my own authority, but he who sent me, the Father, has commanded me what I should say, and what I should declare." (John XII, 46–49) All the students of my time, I feel sure, are ever grateful to Father Miltner for his exposition of the right and marvellous theory of truth to our youthful minds.

17

AFTER SIX YEARS AT HOLY CROSS SEMINARY, MY
dear chums and I, about thirty strong, went
to spend a year at the Novitiate along Saint
Joseph's Lake to brush any and every evil
from our souls. We tried to bury all the vice
beneath the few remaining ruins of the old
building which burned in 1912. I missed Father Irving in the Novitiate, but it was joy to
have Father Miltner as our counsellor, and
also Father William P. Lennartz, a good and
pious priest, as our Novice Master. Among
the many serious duties which fell to our lot
was the building of the new Moreau Seminary, now Saint Joseph Hall. The name Moreau belongs to our saintly founder of the
Congregation of Holy Cross, Father Basil
Moreau.

We pitched right into the construction

work with all the vim and vigor we had. There was among us an old Brother, Joachim by name, who procured sticks of dynamite to blast away and uproot the numerous trees and clear the space for the new house. I can still see the Brother running for his life, when he lighted the fuses. The explosions rocked most of Notre Dame. Crashing timber and long branches littered the ground all over. We had to cut them in pieces with cross-cut saws. Brother Hugh's men hauled them away. Next the foundation had to be dug. This called for spirit and brawn. There were no big motorized bulldozers in those days, so we had to use large iron scoops to pick up the dirt, and pile it up on the wagons pulled by horses. Long shovels were swinging a-plenty until the work was done. Then we moved to the railroad track nearby to unload cars of brick and lumber. With aching hands and tired feet we stacked brick on brick and board on board without minding the heat of the sometimes long hours on sunny and hot

September days. We joined the masons' and carpenters' labor, but not their union. We had a union of our own with headquarters in heaven, and we kept in constant touch with the schedule of prayer in the Novitiate, as we scraped the rust of wickedness by handling the rough brick and sliver-infested boards. When the walls were in shape, and the roof ready, we went up to nail the sheeting. In line like soldiers, bending over for exercise we were pounding with our hammers, until the Novitiate bell, a short distance away, called us to prayer. Brother Columbkill, the chief architect, stone deaf for some time, was among us. He, of course, could not hear the bell. We dropped our tools as one, and proceeded filing off the roof. Brother Columbkill, who was ever anxious to have the building completed as soon as possible, seemed puzzled at our sudden halt in the work and shouted: "What's up?" He quickly provided a pencil and paper, and the one nearest him wrote down the simple message: "time for prayer" for the Brother's benefit. He, in a fit of disgust, let loose something like a lightning bolt of impatience in his definite Irish brogue: "Too Damn Much Prayer!" Brother did not mean what he said. It was a slip of his tongue. He doffed his ancient hat, and piously walked off with us to say his prayers. We laughed off our perspiration, and proceeded on schedule, thrilled at the thought that our new home was almost finished.

Brother Columbkill hired a contractor, a fine gentleman from South Bend. He engineered, supervised the building, and kept his masons and carpenters in good humor. They completed the building almost on time for us to occupy it, after we finished our Novitiate. It was a few years later that I met the daughter of Mr. Marger, Miss Ann Marger, who was an excellent and devoted school nurse, and took care of her father until his death. She told me how her Dad loved to work with us Seminarians in building Moreau Seminary.

Digging trenches for the water and gas

mains from the Novitiate on to the new building was another operation we had to take care of. We worked for days and days with picks and shovels. One very hot afternoon, when we were making the dirt fly all around us, my dear mother happened to be walking along the lake with some friends. Stopping by, my Mom spotted me in what looked like grave-digging clothes. At the sight of me she appeared worried, and immediately concluded that I was killing myself. I consoled her, and assured her: "Mom, here's where they make Notre Dame men out of boys, and every one is guaranteed to live a long life." She was satisfied with this explanation, and parted cheerfully with me. I felt refreshed and stronger after her unexpected visit. My mother died before I became a priest. I felt, then, as if a heavy dark curtain was lowered in front of my life, and I stood very much alone in sorrow and misery. But that is the way it is, when a good mother passes out of this world.

Another chance visitor who appeared at the scene of digging trenches was the beloved Brother André C.S.C. who happened to be at Notre Dame at the time. He came from the Canadian province of our priests and brothers, and had the reputation of being a miracle man who loved Saint Joseph without limits, and fostered devotion to him. A short thin man with an aura of sainthood sparkling over him, he possessed one of those rare natures who for all they are worth undertake the business of humbly making themselves prominent before God. From his face and eyes radiated benediction and goodness that dispelled the shadows of evil. We were all thrilled to put our hands in his. He is up for canonization now, and I hope it comes through soon, so I can truly boast of shaking hands with a saint. Imagination or not, I saw the beautiful sunlight fall in a tiny aureola around his graying head.

We moved to the new seminary in November of 1920. Snow was falling and the temperature was low. Only one side of the house overlooking the lake was really finished. We were cold. A little improvised boiler for the time being hardly provided enough warmth. The cold air combined with the encroaching heat caused the house to be settling in persistent cannonading noises, which annoyed us especially during the hours of the night. It made you believe that a legion of ghosts were making themselves welcome in the new quarters. Ghosts or no ghosts, nothing deterred us from settling down to study and work. The completed chapel was very inviting. We knew where to go to get rid of our troubles and bask in comfort. This holy spot was dedicated to the Sacred Heart to please old Brother Columba who, like Brother André, was on the right track to sainthood. Besides selling footwear in his shop on the campus, he gave out Sacred Heart badges to all his customers and devotees.

Our chapel was in line for a sacristan. I got the assignment and an assistant. We tried to please the Sacred Heart, our Superior and the whole household. Work went on smoothly and pleasantly all along. The first Christmas tree in our chapel has a story. Winter set in early and hard that year, and Christmas was coming in all its glory. A Christmas tree was to be gotten off the grounds. I thought it a good adventure to ride out into the country somewhere around Saint Joseph River, and get one. The weather and the roads were ideal for sleighing, but unfortunately we had no sleigh nor sled, just a worn out wagon and an old horse, a gift from Brother Hugh. We hitched the nag, and started for the Christmas tree, two companions and I. The road, Niles Road, now U.S. 31 North was one of the worst in the country, and then very slippery. We were about a mile out, when the old horse slipped, and sprawled out on the road, harness and all. The icy ground stung his hide aplenty so, much to our surprise, he got up quickly with the harness intact. Giddap, and we proceeded. At the

Four Mile Bridge in South Bend, we got into a deep snow, and Freddie, the horse, snorted and pulled, but to no avail. After one more giant tug, he broke the whipple tree. How to hitch him back to the wagon was a problem. I left my companions to ponder on it, and worry. I went to the ravine close by to look for the Christmas tree. I found a nice one, just the thing to suit my fancy. I was ready to cut it down, when lo and behold, I realized in my absentmindedness from the whipple tree incident, that I had no tools. I had left them in the wagon. The only thing to do first was go back to the wagon to get my saw and hatchet. It was bitter cold, and I was almost freezing to death. Stiffly I climbed up the ravine in view of the road, and what did I see, one of my pals galloping bareback on the old nag. That struck me very funny, in fact it tickled my funny bone to such an extent that I nearly swallowed my floating ribs laughing. The fastest ride on a steed I ever got was on a merry-go-round. But all this

141

paid off. I was getting all warm and comfortable, proving to me that, when you are freezing to death, just laugh heartily, and you will get hot. I surely did, looking at that forlorn "Indiana Cowboy" galloping on Freddie. I soon found out that he was going to the neighboring farmhouse to scare up a whipple tree. In the meantime I went back to the wagon for my saw and hatchet, and assured my other pal that a beautiful tree was waiting for me in the ravine to grace our Christmas holidays. Still full of laughter at the amusing sight on the road, with a reserve of warmth and energy, I mastered my tree for Christmas, and dragged it up to the road. But another surprise! My pals hitched the horse to the wagon, and left for home without me, which, in plain language was a dirty trick. It took me sometime to forgive this lack of consideration and sportsmanship. At any rate, I did not give up on the tree. I tied my saw and hatchet to it, threw it over my shoulders, and put my head through its branches to protect myself from the wind, while a snow storm was really raging. Looking like a camouflaged soldier or a spy, I trudged my way in a bit of comfort and safety from the Four Mile Bridge over a railroad track clear to Notre Dame and our house. What mattered is that I had my beautiful tree to show to my unfair and unsportsmanlike pair of pals. On Christmas morning that tree had a lot of extra meaning for me with the lights flickering on it, as we gathered in the chapel to sing our Christmas carols.

That year it was really a pleasure to welcome spring. It came profusely with verdure and warmth in all its flowering glory. About the middle of it, James Kline, my classmate, and now a venerable and lovable priest, went out for a walk through the farmfields. There in a pasture we ran across a newly-born bullock. He was abandoned and left alone in the field, as the rest of the herd walked off. We took pity on him, and fetched him to our barn which we had built shortly before. He was a tender and a good-looking creature, and we made a resolution to raise him for the primest of beeves. It took some care to feed it. Two fingers dipped in a large pan of milk did the trick. The little bullock ate to its heart's content. When it grew to edible proportions, we had it slaughtered. Brother Leo was looking for it for a long time, and gave him up for lost, but, when he got an invitation from us to attend our Baby Beef feast, he suspected something. The man in the slaughter house did not keep the secret. He told Brother Leo that he killed a bullock for Moreau Seminary, and that the Notre Dame butcher dressed the meat. Brother Leo, however, the fine and condoning gentleman that he was, honored our invitation, congratulated us on our expert handling of his bit of livestock, and cheerfully forgave us.

18

AFTER THE LOST OR STOLEN BULLOCK AND ITS celebration, we go back to the University Visiting lecturers were frequently scheduled. Among them was Dr. James Walsh, one-time Dean of the Fordham Medical School, a philosopher of renown, and author of several books. He was a short, stocky and amusing man, who was always welcome at Notre Dame. He talked common sense, always in a jolly, but very instructive way. He opened one of his lectures by saying that when we get to heaven, three surprises will meet us: one that we finally got there, the second that the people we expected to be there, at least some of them, will not be there, and the third that a lot of folks whom we absolutely counted out of paradise, will be there to greet us. However, said Mr. Walsh with a chuckle, what will it matter, as long as we are sure that we are there. He then drifted to the subject of music, emphasizing an important distinction between soul music and body music, the former created by Almighty God, the latter invented by man. What in music favors the baser passions of man smacks of harmony with the evil spirit. This is most general now. Satan seems to have an alluring baton in it. Uncontrollable passions, like vultures, are preying on the realm of music, stripping it of its gentle and soothing harmony. Soul music evaluates and ennobles the emotions of the soul, body music degrades them. Jazz was the beginning of body music. "Boogie Woogie," a long line of caricatures of tunes followed, and songs such as the Beatles introduced will never have the "charm to soothe a savage beast." These will make it more savage. Dr. Walsh illustrated both kinds of music with his inimitable dancing on the stage that kept the audience in stitches. He proved that music in the word and conduct

of men, women and children to be wholesome and elevating to the character of people, must keep in harmony with God and
Heaven,—a conclusion which is in perfect
accord with that wonderful word, truth,
whose guardian is the Holy Spirit himself.

From Washington Hall, the amusement
auditorium at Notre Dame, we proceed again
to the Grotto. There you would come across
a man, whom you would hardly ever see in
civilian clothes. From first to last he stuck
to his religious habit. He was Father John
Scheir C.S.C., a long-time pastor of Sacred
Heart Church. He also attended to the needs
of the Grotto. He was a plump and amusing
character, who when met, would be first to
greet you. In church he would preach only
ten minutes at a time, saying that he could
give people more in ten minutes than they
could take away. He saw to it that the
candles were always burning at the Grotto
in honor and petition to our Blessed Mother,
while he himself was consuming himself in a
way to give light to those who were willing

to live for Christ in the care of Our Lady. Time and again for serving his Mass, he would tell me to light a candle for my intentions at the Grotto.

Father Scheir, a native of Luxemburg, was also a remarkable teacher of Latin and Greek. He was often interrupted for a moment in his lectures by Father Alexander Kirsch, another Luxemburger, a noted biologist who loved mother nature exceedingly. In the fall of the year he scolded us boys for raking the leaves and burning leaves instead of leaving them on the ground to serve as an excellent fertilizer for the lawn. We always enjoyed his impromptu visits to Father Scheir's classroom. The two were known to us as Jonathan and David. Father Kirsch was the tall Jonathan, and Father Scheir the short David, who could be on target all the time, if not with a sling shot, then with a repartee positively on everything that confronted him. Father Kirsch was more sedate with the bearing of a soldier who would have downed Goliath in a jiffy in a hand-to-hand fight.

Father Scheir's classroom on the first floor of the Main Building was dedicated to the study of Latin and Greek. These languages proved to many a student to be an impregnable stumbling block. There was a fellow among them by the name of John Dearie who took a chance on wrestling Greek. Homer was no friend of his, and he became a miserable failure. Father Scheir smacked his report card with a zero, and a minus one at that. The minus sign in front of the zero was very prominent, so that John Dearie wondered. He came to class, and faced Father Scheir with his report card, objecting: "Father, how come there's a minus sign before that zero?" Father Scheir answered him: "Why, man, don't you know that a zero is something, but a minus zero is absolutely nothing, and that's what you deserve." That was enough to discourage poor John. War was going on at the time, and this student thought it best to enlist in the army. He was still reporting for class. On the day of his departure, he walked very politely to Father

Scheir at his desk, and said: "Good bye, Father, tomorrow I am going into the army." Father Scheir beamed like a general, and reached for his record book: "A hundred per cent for you," he said, "you couldn't beat the Greek, but you will sure beat the German. Congratulations, and God bless you!" John Dearie got the plaudits of the whole class. In the evening Father Scheir and I lighted candles for soldier Dearie at the Grotto.

This added a special charm for me at this shrine of Our Lady. I added one more candle to those I had been burning at the Grotto on different occasions; one usually to the East in preparation for my ordination in four years in Washington, D.C.; one West for my folks at home, and between these right in the middle, one for all at Notre Dame. Our Blessed Mother never let me down, and will fail no one who loves her. It is very sad to hear now about a movement to discredit her, as if her life, sacrifice and tears had nothing to do with our salvation. False theology seeks to obliterate her almost altogether. This is the work of antichrist and the false prophets, against whom Our Lord warned us. Neither man nor the angels can take away Our Mother whom Christ gave to us.

A few years ago on football-game Saturdays you could see a mobile unit heading towards our Grotto. In it was the famous "Boiler Kid," Fred Snite, Jr., who was the victim of that dreaded disease, polio. He was enclosed in a mechanism looking like a boiler to help him breathe. Added to it was his heroic patience and strength, and he lasted a long time in his suffering. All the boost and consolation he needed came from our Grotto.

Some years later on memory lane came a striking appeal to this Grotto from someone who also knew and loved it so well as a student at Notre Dame, Dr. Thomas A. Dooley. After working among the poor and sick people in Asia, he had to yield to a cancerous growth in his body, and lay on his deathbed. It is in this agony that he came in spirit to the Grotto to invoke prayers for a courageous and happy death. Is it not true to say of both

The Grotto, University of Notre Dame

152

these men: "For other sins the scourge they plied, as they the way of penance trod; by prayers and tears they turned aside the wrath of God, till at last the Virgin Queen led them to the mansions in the sky, mansions where the garlands are green and never die." They passed away, thinking of our Grotto at Notre Dame.

Here Dr. Thomas A. Dooley expresses his beautiful lifework in these words:

Listen to the Agony of Asia!
I who am fed,
Who never yet get hungry for a day.
I see the dead,
The children starved for lack of bread
I see, and try to pray.

Listen to the Agony of Asia!
I, who am warm,
Who never yet have lacked the sheltering home
In dull alarm.
The dispossessed of hut and farm
Endlessly and transient roam!

Listen to the Agony of Asia!
I who am strong
In health and laughter in my soul
I see a throng of stunted
Children reared in the wrong,
I want to make them whole.

Listen to the Agony of Asia!
And know full well,
That until I share their bitter cry,
Their pain and hell,
Can God within my spirit dwell
And bring America's blessing nigh!

Well said, Dr. Dooley! The spirit of God dwelt in you. Your noble aid in Asia continues. But, if you are already in Heaven with your fellow-alumnus of Notre Dame, Fred Snite Jr.,—Lovers of our Grotto,—join in our pleading before Our Lady for America. *America is not starving* for lack of food or medicine, but for *lack of religion.* America is in agony, dying spiritually. We like to borrow the merits of your labors, your sacrifices and your sufferings in Asia and elsewhere, and apply them to the wounds of America. We, who know and love God in America, invite you both all over again to crowd among us at the Grotto, and say:

Listen to the Cry of America, you faithful!
You who live in God's holy grace,
And never forget to pray,
For in too many hearts, there, of Religion is
  hardly a trace;
Children with no creed are headed for a
  moral decay.

*

Listen to the Cry of America, you faithful!
You who love the TRUTH divine,
As Christ had told you, His doctrine teach,
And even from the housetops preach,
Shame the godless schools to their decline.

*

Listen to the Cry of America, you faithful!
Nation almost devoid of joy and peace.
Get down before the Grotto of Lourdes on
  both your knees
With hands folded ask Our Lady, bravely,
  to please

155

> *Beg her beloved Son to pour His Grace*
>   *with steady increase.*
>
> ❋
>
> *Wake up to the Cry of America, you faithful!*
> *God will be punishing all crime.*
> *So Hurry! Lift up your hearts and eyes,*
> *And hope for a MIRACLE as a surprise*
> *To this wicked world, from Mary Sublime.*

Lives like those of Dr. Thomas Dooley and Fred Snite Jr. should anchor us permanently and wholeheartedly at the Grotto of the Blessed Virgin. Visions of building another Holy Shrine like the one at Notre Dame materialized in me, and the welcome structure rose to its dedication on the grounds of Saint Stanislaus, Bishop and Martyr Church in South Bend, Indiana for all those who love the Mother of God. From this Grotto MY MIRACLE came. You can not stir me from this belief. In Saint Joseph's Hospital about two years ago when, as I have said before, I struggled for my life, many a good friend of mine was almost sure that the last moments of my earthly pilgrimage had truly arrived. But the good people, who had prayed fervently for me, never for one moment surrendered their precious hope before the health of the sick. Despite the careless on-duty nurse, whom I have already mentioned and forgiven, I awoke from my misery to a new life—a gift from Our Dear Lord from Mary Immaculate. It pays to visit the Grotto for all the graces and favors. Do it on your own sometimes. *Recite your beads!*

It was my privilege also to see the original Grotto at Lourdes, in France in 1950. Beautifully located in the Pyrenees Mountains which unceasingly echo the song, "Ave Maria," it is one spot that you cannot but feel that Mary, the Immaculate Virgin, was there, and is there to welcome every pilgrim in her hidden but sweet and gracious way. The sound of the "Ave Maria" permeates the whole atmosphere and definitely strikes your ears and your heart, even when no one is there, and nobody playing or singing that

The Grotto at Lourdes, France

158

lovable tune. During the intervals the echoes remain, and never fade or die. The stone on which The Virgin Lady stood, while she appeared to Saint Bernadette, has been touched by human hands and kissed by human lips to an unbelievable smoothness, to which I added a touch and a kiss, unworthy, but prayfully mine. I have tried to remember every person I ever have known, when I was all alone at the Holy Shrine at Lourdes.

WHAT A PIECE OF WORK IS MAN! HOW NOBLE IN reason! how noble in faculty! in form and moving how express and admirable! in action how like an angel! in apprehension how like a God! the beauty of the world! the paragon of animals! This epitome on man in general found in Shakespeare's Hamlet offers us an opportunity to speculate just who in particular would fit all the way in this eulogy. To my mind there are many individuals I met in life, who could portray this ideal, but now for me there is one outstanding example, a man who also loved our Grotto to an almost heroic degree. He was the one priest among us who exclusively reached the dignity of a Prince of the Church, His Eminence Cardinal John O'Hara. He was really a piece of the work of God, personable, brilliant, an angel before man, an ace in the beauty of Notre Dame. He was kindness personified, and above all humble. No one knew this better than his beloved students, when he mingled among them as a young priest.

Father O'Hara became the president of the university, and after a brilliant career in that office, the Holy Pontiff appointed him to the Military Ordinariate of the Armed Forces of the United States, then to Bishop of Buffalo, New York, and finally to Archbishop and Cardinal of Philadelphia, Pennsylvania. Everywhere he applied good judgement, ingenuity and sagacity, all of which proved that he had the unlimited faculty to do things right, the way God wanted him to do. He moved from place to place on the path of virtue, so that the admiration usually reserved for the angels began taking hold of him. Under his instruction, guidance and counsel many a man, woman and child was actually steeled in Christianity and Catholicism.

I liked Father O'Hara in the classroom. He was an all-round professor of history of the United States. He had the inimitable knack of describing the chronicles of our country briefly and always to the point. His class sessions were an inspiration to a high degree of patriotism. It was a pleasure to listen to him. From George Washington's simple story of the cherry tree to his Cross-

161

ing of the Delaware, and from Lincoln's log cabin to his Gettysburg Address, what was happening seemed to be living in Father O'Hara's words. You could spend the severe winter with George Washington at Valley Forge, and join Abe Lincoln in splitting rails at his log cabin. Here I developed a most profound fondness especially for the character of Abraham Lincoln. A cherished dream was born. A few years later, I had the fortune to be on the spot where Lincoln delivered his Gettysburg Address, and in Ford's Theatre in Washington, D.C., where he lost his life. On one beautiful summer afternoon in Springfield, Illinois, I bowed my head right at Lincoln's tomb, thinking: "He tried to be all things to all men." He made a noble and the right appraisal of the negro. He looms in our history as the Great Emancipator, and truly so, for he conceived and nurtured a godlike sympathy all his own, for the colored man. He grieved over the unfair attitude of the Southern bosses toward the negro. After he had done away with slavery, he was intent upon finding somewhere in the world a colony suitable exclusively for the American blackman to stem and forestall any further degradation and insult to genuine human beings. Fearing that this could not be done immediately, that the Southern mind would not surrender readily the racial degradation and the misery of the colored folk, he pondered over setting them apart with American help and protection. Otherwise, as he put it, *the racial question* would in time assume improper and insurmountable proportions. People will be groping in the dark, as it were, for a proper solution. We are well aware of what we are facing right now. After a century and four years since Lincoln's death, his prophecy registers true. We need someone with the genius of Abraham Lincoln to free this country, presumably Christian, from the ravages of misunderstanding and prejudice. Lincoln once made this remark: "Die, when I may, I want it said by those

163

who know me best, that I always plucked a thistle and planted a flower, where a flower would grow." In Cardinal O'Hara's mind, as in one who knew Lincoln best, that flower of understanding, sympathy, encouragement and proper education for the negro grew, and it must blossom in all the people, now and for all time.

I should like to return to Father O'Hara again as a young priest. Outside of his classroom, he was a big brother to all boys, teaching them by word and example to look for and toward the things of God first and foremost. He urged them especially to rely on their Holy Mass and Holy Communion. Therein he assured them, they would find help, comfort and peace. It should not be any different now. Our Lord is the same. He did not change, and will not ever change.

20

THERE WERE ANY NUMBER OF MEN OF GOD WHO walked these grounds, when Notre Dame was nearing its century mark. Father Daniel Hudson who celebrated his fiftieth year as editor of his beloved periodical, the *Ave Maria*, and also the golden jubilee of his priesthood, all along gave you the impression that a dearer person had never been born. To come across him was very close to meeting an angel in human form. He is best described in the "Memoirs" of him by Father John W. Cavenaugh, his fellow priest, as a man with an unwrinkled face, with a close-trimmed white Van Dyke beard matching his pointed pompadour snow-white hair, and large gray-blue eyes upturned to heaven. His strong hands clasped the rosary, as he walked up and down very often in front of the Grotto in spring, summer, fall and in wintertime well bundled up.

> *"Numb were this beadsman's fingers while*
> *   he told*
> *His Rosary, while his frosted breath*
> *Like pious incense from a censer old*
> *Seemed taking flight for Heaven without*
> *   a death,*
> *Past the sweet Virgin's statue, while his*
> *   prayers he saith."*

When I was at Lourdes in France, the idea of the presence of the Blessed Virgin being there permeated me completely. Some such feeling, I recalled, overwhelmed me, when I stood face to face with Father Hudson. When he was preaching each year on the last of April, to give a start to the May Devotions in Sacred Heart Church, a very elderly priest of our Congregation, Father Timothy Maher by name, made this friendly observation, for he loved Father Hudson very much: "Hudson is just like a little rooster." There is a lot of wisdom in this playful remark, for what this venerable man of God meant was that his good friend was crowing for the Blessed Virgin to the end of love, and he really had someone to crow about. And, if we follow up this word "crow" today, about the only thing that the Virgin Mother of God, perfect in all respects before the Holy Trinity and man, would need is to be more and more "crowed about" in the face of the rumors that fly about that she can fade away as one no longer needed in our spiritual life. Whoever says that, pronounce him with Saint Paul, an anathema.

Father Hudson, as editor of the *Ave Maria*, wrote for fifty years for the young and the old to keep before the eyes of the Catholic and even non-Catholic people the greatest human being that ever lived, *Mary, The Immaculate Conception*. He had displayed in prose and poetry her humility and her power of intercession for us before Almighty God. When it comes to the need of our spiritual make-up, we can always count on her. Father Hudson brought a great number of converts to our faith by "crowing," if we may use the word, about the Blessed Virgin. He, once dubbed as a "Little Rooster" outcrowed everybody in the world.

What an honor it was to have him as a dear friend. From his own lips I have learned of his remarkable and sincere thoughtfulness spread like rays of sunshine over all humanity. He loved all people, children and especially the nuns. He gave them all the credit for their utmost piety and for their educating the little ones in first of all the love of God. Most of the devoted Sisters he talked about are now in heaven, praying and singing for us. What an enormous calamity it is today that the number of these Sisters is rapidly diminishing among us, simply because the immaculate Mother of God is not loved as she should be.

Father John W. Cavenaugh was a one-time President of Notre Dame, and a bosom pal of Father Hudson. It was a case of two geniuses understanding each other. Father Cavenaugh was often described as the eagle with the golden tongue, who soaring on to the great heights of wisdom, could pick you up to go along with him on the splendid wings of his oratory. We at Notre Dame enjoyed and appreciated every one of his scholarly and uplifting speeches. If you had been sports-minded, you would have to admit that Father Cavenaugh by his executive power and persuasive oratory was in a great part responsible for the great victory over the Army in that football game of 1913. This particular event opened a new and broad vista for all other illustrious achievements brought to the feet of the Lady of the Golden Dome.

Shortly before my graduation I met Father Cavenaugh walking up and down in our cemetery, whispering his prayers for our beloved dead. I interrupted him with my greeting. He responded quickly in his usual jovial manner. When I reminded him that this was my senior year, he, who knew me well, showered his more than ordinary congratulations on my being a graduate of Notre Dame, and in the course of our little talk, he added this question: "How on earth did you get by Notre Dame with that long name of yours?" "Because," I said, "I have loved the Irish, and the Irish loved me." I could not have hit on a better answer, for he was mighty pleased, and gave me his generous blessing. Before we parted, we mentioned our mutual friend, dear Father Hudson, and we agreed that not for love nor money would this holy priest ever leave the grounds for anything. But in later years both Father Cavenaugh and I were proven wrong.

When I was ordained a priest, Father Hudson, for the first time, as many who knew him well remarked, left Notre Dame to be present at my first Solemn Mass, and came to my home for our little celebration. That was something unbelievable, when news spread abroad that this gem of a father left his sanctum, and hung his hat in my home. I have been ever grateful to him for that, because he filled, as no one else could, the void of absence of my dear Father and Mother. Father Hudson loved the priesthood, and he told me how happy he was that it came to me. Father Hudson, I will never amount to much, but you are forever on the honor role where I put you, in the Hall of Fame at Notre Dame.

ALL THINGS COME FROM ALMIGHTY GOD EVEN the small and insignificant, like the ant, the cricket, the wren and the ever present sparrow, so also the big and important, the great and marvellous, like human life, home building, aviation, and all recreation facilities. It is good to think that God is just everything to us. But did you ever consider that there is something which transcends all you can think of, and that is the exclusive and the grandest thing among the grand, the holy priesthood. How long can you live as a priest? As long as anybody else, who takes care of himself, but, you as a priest, must live here as a priest to the end of your life, because what you have in you is eternal, and must be returned unsullied to Almighty God to save your soul.— *Sacerdos in aeternum—*

To be happy, to have good friends, to cultivate a good appetite, and above all to have a clear conscience is to get along in life. You might supplement this with a very simple philosophy, coming from an old West Virginia mountaineer, whom I met, as he trudged along happily one morning in the beautiful Shenandoah Valley. This is where we camped for three summers, while we were students in Washington, D.C.—"How-dee, Uncle Buck, and how are you today?" I greeted the mountaineer. "Right smart," he answered, "and why shouldn't I be? I love God, cheat the devil, mind my own business and keep my bowels moving." That is the way he was reaching a ripe old age.

To grow in this world is something everybody is slated to do. To know how to grow gracefully is a masterpiece of wisdom. You are not here to store and store earthly things and boast of a great wealth, but to live accumulating an unlocked treasury of health, good will, kindness, cheerfulness and above all God's grace, by which others will learn to acquire it for themselves to advance in age beautifully, cheerfully and peacefully. Father Cornelius Hagerty, my dear friend at Notre Dame now, is a shining example of one still growing in age, wisdom and grace before God and man. He is pushing well toward ninety years. He was blessed with a rugged body, destined to be a thorough outdoor as well as an indoor man. In the classroom he was a first-rate philosopher instructing and explaining others unto the truth, and holding doggedly to IT. In the world of field and stream he has been an explorer and a lover of nature in all its forms. You could see him outside school hours playing baseball or plying his canoe, cooking out of doors and sporting always with topnotch genial friends. He stands out for me in his long youthful days as a fulfillment of the axiom: a healthy body in a sound and healthy soul, sound with the grace of God shining in his face. The weight of his brawny shoulders was usually taken off the shoulders of others on to his own. What he has been doing for God reflects in the love and honor he has for his fellowmen. I love to recall this incident which happened in Father Cornelius's life.

Some years ago a middle-aged Sister of the Holy Cross was stricken for some time with a mental illness. She slipped by the cautious eyes of those who cared for her, and ran away to hurl herself down over an embankment into the Saint Joseph River and drowned. The problem was to find her body. When Father Cornelius heard of the tragedy, he took it upon himself to tackle this unusual, fear-provoking and perhaps scandal suggesting task to people who would not think just right. The Sister of the Holy Cross in her habit was without a shadow of doubt perfectly innocent. She was somebody consecrated to God, and had to be honored as such, thought Father Cornelius. He did not hesitate to take action, for this one important act of mercy. Fitting out his canoe, he took with him a trusty companion and set out to find the body of the victim. He paddled the canoe up and down the river day and night, while all the Sisters at the convent at Saint Mary's prayed. It did not take very long that Father Cornelius reverently brought the body to shore to the astonishment of all concerned. It was his up-to-the-minute good judgement and strength, his determination, perseverance and hope that completed this blessed act of mercy. It is but one of the numerous of his good deeds for which on his last day Father Cornelius will draw this worthy assurance: "Well done, good and faithful servant, because you have done this for the least of my little ones, you have done it unto me. Enter into the kingdom of God."

THE MOST IMPORTANT PEOPLE AT NOTRE DAME were always the priests and the Brothers. They are now, by some form of modern philosophy and theology minus of the genuine truth, being deprived of their rank and prerogative. Let it be understood for all time that nobody, but nobody, can adequately replace a priest except another honest-to-goodness priest. Where there is a good priest, there is God. And God must be ever at Notre Dame. It is an added blessing from Almighty God that where there are good priests, there are also good Brothers to second the priests in their work and prayer to save souls for God and heaven.

There is one more thing to remember,—to remember once for all and for good,—and that is for all priests, Sisters and Brothers, and for all the Catholic men, women, and children to understand that they, without any hesitation, *ought to obey* our Holy Father, the Pope, who like Saint Peter and every one of his genuine successors, *is the rightly constituted representative of and spokesman for Jesus Christ, our Lord, the king of heaven and earth.*

If you should enter the Sacred Heart Church at Notre Dame on one of the great Catholic Feasts, you would notice a somewhat diminutive priest, vested in cassock and surplice, kneeling very attentively in one of the front pews. He is the oldest priest in our Congregation of Holy Cross, a priest of short stature, who, when he was young, was exiled from France, his native land in 1903. He came to Notre Dame with several of his confrères, forced to leave France on account of the persecution of the Religious there at that time. He was ordained here, and has spent most of his 60 priestly years teaching very devotedly and regularly. At four score and seven summers he meets you always with a cheery smile, and is sure of catching every word you say. His ears are not dull, and his eyes not dim for his age. His wits are anything but slow. He can bring you interesting memories to the fore,—galore to excite your curiosity with a hankering for more. He is a dynamo for holy sympathy, and can perk you up remarkably, when your spirits are low.

What did he do at Notre Dame outside of his teaching hours, and what does he do now, when he is retired from the classroom? You can still see him walking around our blessed lakes among the bushes and flowers, stopping now and then to feed the many wild ducks, as they wing their way and splash down on the water, swimming to fix their continual abode on the little islands. From there they float in flocks to welcome their friend, this Father, who has something for them to enjoy every time they meet him at the shore. A pet attraction for him also has been the flocks of athletes on the playing fields. He has been up on almost all the games at Notre Dame, cheering and praying for the teams to win in all the sports. By his good advice and encouragement to many an athlete, he planted a Monogram on the students' chests. In fact they voted one for him to wear. Familiar with French cuisine, he specializes all along in culinary art. He can roast a duck, retrieved from the lake to a king's taste, and supply all the trimmings by himself alone, of course.

But all in all, what you admire in him is his constant courage in carrying the Cross of Christ. His life is like a long drawn-out symphony whose charm penetrates all corners at Notre Dame. What makes me think of that? It is his name—Father Charles L. Doremus, the first syllables of which sound out the diatonic musical scale, Do, Re, Mi.—Add the remaining five and you make it complete as a keynote to his life, which has been a pleasant and most useful contribution to his Alma Mater, Notre Dame.

Doremus:

Do—He goes about like Christ did on earth, always doing good.

Re—Receives everybody kindly in sunshine, rain and snow any day.

Mi—Minds his own business, which is the business of God, being ever eager to make every one a Disciple of Our Lord just like he is.

Fa—Far advanced in years, he remains YOUNG AT HEART. At times his spryness will remind you of a robin in spring.

Sol—What a soul!

La—OOH, la, la! How do you go on, Father?

Ti—To a T he is sincere even to the core of his heart itself!

Do—THAT IS FATHER CHARLES L. DORE-MUS at 87. Blessed are they who ease the days for him on his journey HOME in loving ways.

FOR A MOMENT NOW WE PAUSE TO CONSIDER AN epochal dream come true to a young man in May 1927. As a budding aviator, he took off in a monoplane called the *Spirit of St. Louis,* and flew all alone across the Atlantic Ocean from New York to Paris. "I am Charles Lindbergh," he said as crowds of the French people surrounded his landing plane. He stood out among them as "America's Lone Eagle," who had accomplished what no other human being ever did. He dared to span the ocean in a solo flight, and added this remarkable feat to the progress of the fast moving science of aviation. We Americans were joined by the rest of the world in shouting his acclaim. We heard of his cheerful landing on the air field in France through the Radio. Television had not made its debut as yet. We saw the remarkable pictures of this historical event in newsreels and various periodicals. Recognition and honors kept heaping upon the well-deserving Charles Lindbergh, now a Colonel, and forever an All American Hero.

Forty-two years later, we come upon another giant dream of dreams—*our fellow Americans flying to the moon.* Yes, on Sunday July 20, 1969, *our men really landed on the moon, and unfurled the United States flag there.* Sooner than we expected our latest *spacecraft, the Apollo 11,* made up of two modules, the Columbia and the Eagle, blasted off under the guiding providence of Almighty God on its epic journey to the moon. On the fifth day in orbit the Apollo 11 landed cautiously and gently on the lunar surface.

The Columbia, carrying as its pilot Michael Collins, the one of the three fliers aboard, parted with the two other human "Eagles," and continued most accurately in its orbit, while the whole earth was overpowered with wonder and excitement. In the meantime Neil Armstrong in command, and Edwin Aldrin Jr. left behind, labored gallantly upon the ladder of their module to come down and set first one foot and then the other on the moon. They succeeded and extended their greetings as well as ours to the "EMPRESS OF THE NIGHT" by unfurling for her the flag of the United States. Neil Armstrong then voiced what will remain outstanding among the greatest historic utterances for all ages to come: "This one step for a man, but one giant leap for mankind."

If the moon were really a lady, she would have accepted this grand salutation with open arms, as we with eager eyes and joyful hearts watched intensely the whole procedure on the marvel of television. But her Sky-all Highness simply shed her usual topmost brilliance, casting her soft beams to spread her beauty and welcome all over our trees and flowers, everything else and everybody on the earth far below. We kept on looking at our heroes as their fabulous preparation and uncanny skill were now taking effect in their marvellous exploration of the moon.

All Hail to our brave astronauts! Ages ago, when Julius Caesar commandingly faced the Black Sea, and visualized to his advantage the countries surrounding it, he made this famous remark: "I came, I saw, I conquered." We reverse one word of his triumphal expression for our astronauts: they conquered, they came, they saw, they walked on the moon, and they opened the outer space for further conquests.

We saw them at close range. God bless our astronauts, and all who mapped their outstanding space flight. For this we thank God sincerely! We will fly the Star Spangled Banner more proudly than ever, knowing that now our Flag rests on top of the Moon.

After this wonderful lunar exploration was over, the Columbia came back to pick up Neil Armstrong and Edwin E. Aldrin Jr. Welcoming his buddies aboard the Eagle, unscathed and triumphant all three headed on schedule for Mother Earth. After four more days in flight they splashed down into the sea. We bailed them out from the unkind turbulence of waters, and got them safely home.—They have left their footprints, and pinned, as it were, *their priceless gem of American courage* on the shining breast of her highness, the moon. All in all they have enriched our American life.

Beyond all this earthly jubilation there is

something that strikes one's mind, as we honor our intrepid heroes. They are red-blooded Americans of the ordinary stock whose hard work and predilection guided their feet to set on the surface of the moon, but believe it or not, they were actually *not the first to touch the surface of the moon.* Long, long ago there was an extraordinary human being who stood on the moon as queen of heaven and earth: "A woman clothed with the sun and the *moon was under her feet,* and on her head a crown of twelve stars," according to Chapter XII, verse 1 of the Apocalypse of St. John. By accommodation the Church applies this passage to no one else but the Blessed Virgin Mary, Mother of God, with all her gracious love and care for us. Therefore, she it was who first set her feet upon the moon. Cast all your anxiety upon her, for she looks upon you and loves you, as long as you are on this earth.

HAVE A BONNIE WISH FOR EVERYBODY. IF YOU ever visit the Grotto at Saint Stan's Parish in South Bend, Indiana, right near this Holy Shrine you will find a Wishing Well also dedicated to Our Blessed Mother. Stop there a moment, and recite this prayer:

Our Lady of the Wishing Well!
Grant me my wish for love of God, good
*   health, good luck and neighbors' love.*
And peace for this old world with guidance
*   from above.*

Wishing Well, St. Stanislaus Parish, South Bend

Give us all courage to stand the trials of
    passing years
In sunshine and rain with smiles and tears
Like our forefathers did with blessings
    from You in many different ways
In the good, old horse-and-buggy days!

LOOKING INTO A BLESSED FUTURE, MAY ALL
YOUR CHERISHED DREAMS COME TRUE!

Father Jan.
Class of 1922